For God + Country!

THE ASSAULT ON
AMERICA

Harrison House

Shippensburg, PA

ALEX McFARLAND

THE ASSAULT ON
AMERICA

HOW TO DEFEND OUR NATION
BEFORE IT'S TOO LATE

© Copyright 2020 – Alex McFarland

Printed in the United States of America. All rights reserved. No portion of this book may be reproduced, stored in a retrieval system, or transmitted in any form or by any means—electronic, mechanical, photocopy, recording, scanning, or other—except for brief quotations in critical reviews or articles, without the prior written permission of the publisher. Scripture quotations marked NKJV are taken from the New King James Version®. Copyright © 1982 by Thomas Nelson, Inc. Used by permission. All rights reserved. Scripture quotations marked NIV are from THE HOLY BIBLE, NEW INTERNATIONAL VERSION®, NIV® Copyright © 1973, 1978, 1984, 2011 by Biblica, Inc.™ Used by permission. All rights reserved worldwide. Scripture quotations marked NASB are from the NEW AMERICAN STANDARD BIBLE®, Copyright © 1960, 1962, 1963, 1968, 1971, 1972, 1973, 1975, 1977, 1995 by The Lockman Foundation. Used by permission. Scripture quotations marked KJV are from the King James Version. Scripture quotations marked HCSB are from the Holman Christian Standard Bible®, Copyright © 1999, 2000, 2002, 2003, 2009 by Holman Bible Publishers. Used by permission. Holman Christian Standard Bible®, Holman CSB®, and HCSB® are federally registered trademarks of Holman Bible Publishers. Scripture quotations marked ESV are from The Holy Bible, English Standard Version (ESV) and is adapted from the Revised Standard Version of the Bible, copyright Division of Christian Education of the National Council of the Churches of Christ in the U.S.A. All rights reserved.

Published by Harrison House Publishers
Shippensburg, PA 17257

Cover design by Eileen Rockwell

ISBN 13 TP: 978-1-6803-1733-6

ISBN 13 eBook: 978-1-6803-1734-3

ISBN HC: 978-1-6803-1736-7

ISBN LP: 978-1-6803-1735-0

For Worldwide Distribution, Printed in the USA

1 2 3 4 5 6 7 8 / 24 23 22 21 20

CONTENTS

Appendices

FOREWORD

The United States is at a crossroads, and it burdens me greatly. As a nation we have turned our back on God and have pursued the things of this world instead.

I'm reminded of 2 Kings, chapter 22. King Josiah led a campaign to repair the Jewish temple; and as they were working on the project, the carpenters stumbled upon an interesting old scroll. As they read through it, the men realized that they were holding the nearly-forgotten Scriptures of the True and Living God.

Hilkiah, who was Israel's high priest at the time, reported to the king that they had "found the Book of the Law in the temple of the Lord." It's a sad irony and commentary that God's Word was right there in God's temple all along, yet even the priests had lost track of it.

At the king's command, the newly rediscovered Book of the Covenant was read publicly, and something amazing happened. As the Word of God was proclaimed, people repented and turned back to the Lord, and a great revival came!

We need this in America today! I pray for the Holy Spirit to bring this country to a state of repentance like we read about in 2 Kings.

The Assault on America—How to Defend Our Nation Before It's Too Late shares this theme. The problems that individual people and our country face seem endless. But there is a wonderful solution for all people, regardless of their situation or background—a new life through a relationship with Jesus Christ.

Jesus alone holds the answer to the problems that plague us. He offers the hope, peace, purpose, love, joy, and redemption that seem so elusive today.

Alex McFarland's explanation of the current spiritual condition of America is timely, and his call for people to put their faith in Jesus is clear and compelling. I encourage you to thoughtfully read *The Assault on America,* and share it with a friend.

I also encourage you to pray for revival in America and beyond. Even in the midst of increasing darkness, God is moving in remarkable ways in this present age.

May God bless you and use you as a bold witness for Christ!

—Will Graham, Vice President
Billy Graham Evangelistic Association
www.billygraham.org

SAVING THE IRREPLACEABLE

Have you ever been at a party where the group played a "What if?" conversational game? At several gatherings over the years, I've participated in many of these get-to-know-your-neighbor ice breakers. One common question I've heard is, "If your house was on fire and you could run in and only grab one thing, what would it be?"

How would you answer that question? Virtually all adults will say something like their pictures or photo albums. I've heard some say they would grab their Bible, and it always moved my heart on the one or two occasions when people have somberly said that they would grab their marriage certificate.

If a person's house was burning down, why wouldn't they grab the flat screen TV? That probably cost more than a bunch of faded old photos. Why have people run through flames to make sure all of the children are located, to rescue their pet, or even carry out a fishbowl when things like jewelry and electronics are much more valuable? It is because some things in this world are *irreplaceable*. We will risk our lives for precious things which, if lost, could never be acquired again. And we should. Some things in this world are worth much more than money. In fact, some things are worth dying for.

This book is about rescuing some things that may be rapidly and irretrievably lost.

1

HAS AMERICA REACHED ITS EXPIRATION DATE?

Walking around the smoldering ruins of Ground Zero less than two days after 9/11 was not something I would exactly call a "privilege." But the experiences of those days are times I will never forget. Though sad and somber, it was an honor to be serving as part of a ministry team in the immediate aftermath of the terrorist attacks. We counseled individuals blindsided by grief, prayed with hundreds of New York's first responders, and listened to the stories of people from every imaginable background.

As news outlets commented round the clock on the attacks, many of the stories analyzed the physics of how the World Trade Center Towers fell:

- The planes crashed into the buildings, instantly spewing thousands of gallons of jet fuel everywhere.
- Fire engulfed nearly 10 floors in each building on impact, first in the North Tower, and then in the South.

- Two buildings that had taken eight years to construct lay on the ground in rubble just 56 minutes from impact (South Tower) and after 102 minutes (North Tower).

The trifecta of physical destruction began as the hijacked jets breached the Towers' concrete and metal exterior, weakening the structure overall. Intense heat from burning jet fuel compromised and eventually melted steel support beams throughout several floors. The incalculable weight of floors above points of impact was, tragically, mass enough to crush everything below.

The awful spectacle of the Towers' fall (and the destruction of entire city blocks of buildings and property nearby) is acutely painful to watch even two decades later. The deaths of more than 2,700 people, the loss of feeling safe on American soil, and the omnipresent sway of Islamic terrorism has caused the world to feel since 9/11 changed life to a degree that overstatement is near impossible.

At Risk of Extinction?

Just as multiple contributing factors coalesced into the falling of the Towers, the combination of several detriments is bringing down (what was) the greatest nation on earth—the United States of America. The pathological irony in the case of our unraveling nation is that three dynamics key to the preservation of America are being actively suppressed and opposed.

Family, Morality, and Human Life

Far too many high-profile influencers can't be counted on to take unflinching stances for marriage and family, objective truth, and moral accountability, nor for the sacredness of life and human rights. Elected officials, public educators, and celebrities prattle endlessly about rights, but virtually always from a perspective of moral relativism. We hear, "It is my right to marry whomever or whatever I choose," or, "It is my right to define my gender for myself," or, "It is my right to have an abortion." These "rights" are assumed and asserted. Meaningful discussion to the contrary is rarely allowed.

Suppressed and Opposed in Education

American public education has been overwhelmingly secularized for several generations. It is hardly mysterious why most Gen Xers, Millennials, and those younger reject Christianity, traditional family structures, morals, and patriotism, or are clueless about such things altogether. Public education is programmed to crank out masses of compliant little socialists. We are uploading our kids with vacuous, bankrupt, unlivable philosophies, and this will ultimately mean the loss of our Constitution if it does not stop.

It has been at least four decades since high school diplomas and college degrees represented a type of promise that graduates had learned to truly think, live morally, and to cherish our nation. The left fights hard against school choice because public classrooms have been blinding young minds from content about morals and patriotism, if not steering them away completely.

Suppressed and Opposed in Entertainment

Pop media and the entertainment industry pulse out imagery and narrative that captures, or at least greatly influences, the imaginations of all ages. Again, with rare exception, values that contribute to the weakening of our society are repeated and reinforced. From the latest blockbuster film, the uber-liberal pages of *Rolling Stone*, to the logic-bereft desk of *The View*, leftist views about sexuality, family, religion, and politics are endlessly echoed.

Volumes of data affirm the positive outcomes, long and short term, of what are called "traditional values." Described favorably or dismissively, depending who you're listening to, "traditional values" are at the core of the battle for our nation's future. Notice, however, an irony regarding those who would have us redefine marriage, relativize morality, reimagine gender, and thoroughly revise America. The very same influencers who reprehend traditional values have a platform and enjoy prosperity due to those values.

The Atlantic published an insightful piece several years ago titled, "Why is it Hard for Liberals to Talk about 'Family Values'?" The essay pointed out that for all of the pontifications about the oppressiveness of marriage and the need for sexual liberation, "...stable marriage and community are the secret sauce of economic well-being that nobody on the left wants to admit to using."[1]

The left's stance that traditional social structures are inherently oppressive and "bad"—a presupposition held to, defended, and enforced for decades—makes for impassioned talking points. But successful, influential Democrat progressives do not live this way, nor do they encourage their kids, if they have them, to do so. But they're quieter about the ways that traditional "family values" are guiding their own choices.

Democratic candidates advocate for leftist/progressive policy positions with lockstep predictability. Ironically, the affluence and social standing enjoyed by liberal leaders came about in the context of "traditionally married," two-parent households. In other words, Dems "talk it" but they don't "live it." Research documents that economic success is directly tied to family stability.[2]

Ronald Reagan famously said that government programs, once enacted, never "die." Our 40th President joked that government programs and agencies are "the closest thing to eternal life" seen on this planet. Perhaps that is why the left so tenaciously continues to build its platforms of demonstrably flawed planks.

Though career politicians on the left would hardly admit it, responsible government really does have a vested interest in promoting what our Founders (and those who influenced them) would call, "the virtues." According to Federalist writer Alexander Hamilton, true social justice is experienced only when objective morality (commonly referred to as, our "Judeo-Christian heritage," or simply called, "the Ten Commandments") is assumed. Over time, our pervasive belief in God, morality and personal accountability, and consistently a high view of human life has resulted in what philosophers call, "the good."

But God, family, personal accountability, sexual abstinence until marriage, self-restraint, patriotism, absolute morality—these are all things that the left incites each new generation to fight against. They have successfully imparted their viewpoints to millions. Yet it is impossible to argue that morally and socially our nation is better off for the left's decades-long campaign of "progressivism." As Matt Walsh observes in his book *Church of Cowards*:

Homosexuals, far from being called to purity, are encouraged to "marry" each other. Raucous parades are held across the country to applaud sodomy. Perversion is promoted and advertised everywhere. The heathens see that some of the men here in this Christian country dress in skirts and pretend to be women, and everyone else plays along with the charade. They see drag queen story hours at libraries, cross-dressing child models on television, and many other forms of debauchery—all tolerated and even celebrated.[3]

Teddy Roosevelt on the Decline of France

Some 30 years after Tocqueville wrote *Democracy in America*, published works coming from the man who would become our 26th President consistently demonstrated a keen understanding of what made for the success of this nation. In Theodore Roosevelt's analysis of America, he contrasted our history with that of another, not-so-fortunate people, the French during the period leading up to their revolution. Roosevelt noted that France, in the years that would coalesce into social and political overthrow, was a place of great impiety. "They did not believe anything," Roosevelt wrote.

He cites American revolutionary Gouverneur Morris (who had written to General Washington regarding the conditions in 18th century France): "There is an utter prostration of morals, but this general proposition can never convey to an American mind the degree of depravity....

The great mass of common people have no religion but their priests, no law but their superiors, no morals but their interest."[4]

In chronicling the birth of America, documenting parts of its early history, and championing what he saw as its superiority to other nations, Roosevelt frequently warned of things that he saw as threats to the country: loss of God, loss of morality, loss of national spirit, absence of decisiveness and conviction. Roosevelt saw these deficiencies for the threats that they are. What would Roosevelt say about college professors today, that majority of whom identify as politically liberal and spiritually agnostic? What would he think of the left removing his own statue from the American Museum of Natural History, with a CNN writer noting, "Removing the Teddy Roosevelt statue is just the beginning"?[5] Loss of morals, loss of family, and loss of reverence for human life have been the undoing of cultures ancient and modern.

Knowing this, why are Dems, influencers, and other leaders zealously hanging on to policies that are causing, and will continue to cause, further national erosion? *Why?* Leaders who care about this country should advocate for moral truth and personal accountability, and for a high view of life. Anyone who speaks out against the prevailing relativist/hedonist/socialist narratives will need courage, confidence, and resilience. Do you have these?

Political correctness be damned; we're talking about America's survival and human thriving.

Where Are We Headed?

Liberal-progressive ideas are contributing to the weakening of our culture, and the tide must turn if our Constitution and its liberties are to be preserved. Leftist powers have held majority sway in politics, education, and culture for decades. Dare we hope that someone within the ranks of Democratic leadership has the moral courage to ask, "Why are we continuing down this toxic path?"

Whether the hope for a moral awakening among Democrats would be justified, only God knows. But since we're on the subject of God, let's pray to Him that liberal demagogues will not only experience an epiphany but would also turn back from their systematic demolition of America.

Is This the End?

Surreal doesn't even begin to describe the scene. It was an evening I will never forget.

It was about 8:30 p.m. on a Saturday night, and I and the group with me had spent nearly three hours in the police station. This was not just any police station—we were in one of the most famous cities in the world—Jerusalem! Our tour group had been robbed. Cell phones, laptops, and wallets were gone, but most troubling of all, many of us had been relieved of our U.S. passports.

There in the office, the police chief was speaking with investigating officers, staff, and our group members. For over a week we had been in Jerusalem, all of us deeply stirred, walking where Jesus had once walked. But even the most awestruck spiritual pilgrim becomes singularly focused when they're 5,000 miles from home and in our situation. The one question on our minds, was, "How can we get a new passport?"

The Jerusalem police were extremely helpful. Though our possessions were not recovered, they did get us to the U.S. embassy and helped with temporary IDs and other needs. The Jewish officers were empathetic and reassuring during the process. They sensed our anxiety and talked with us encouragingly. One officer asked about my occupation and I told him I taught apologetics at a university. "Apologetics? What is that?" he asked. I explained that apologetics deals with evidence for the Bible. "So, you teach theology?"

"Well, yes, that's part of it," I replied.

Cutting his eyes left and right, the officer leaned toward me, asking in almost a whisper, "What about the end of time? Do you believe God, uh, Jesus will truly come back?"

The holy city is no place for the unholy act some street thieves did to us. But getting to talk with an officer about what Scripture says regarding the end times made the hassle a little more bearable. He seemed deeply interested in learning more about this question. Increasingly, I find he is not alone. Many are asking, has our world—or has America—reached its expiration date?

The Bible has a lot to say regarding the culmination of history and the final judgment of all people—and much about the end times we learn from the words of Jesus Christ. As the COVID-19 situation has enveloped the globe, and as the impact on all our lives has ranged from hours not worked, wages lost, to increasing shortages at the grocery, anxiety is only growing. People are scared, economies are crumbling, and many rightly wonder, "Just how permanent is the loss of civil liberties COVID-19 is creating?" Online and on-air, our organization is daily receiving numerous inquiries about how close humanity might be to the end times, and specifically, to the return of Christ.

Why are so many people discussing the end of our world as we know it? What will be some of the precursors to Jesus' return? Will America even exist by the time of "the world's end"? The Bible lays out at least ten areas to consider when answering the question regarding the last days, and whether America has reached its expiration date. Signs that we may be near the end of history:

1. The growth of the Christian church.

"This gospel of the kingdom shall be preached the whole world as a testimony to all the nations, and then the end will come" (Matthew 24:14 NASB).

2. Increase in evil.

"Iniquity shall abound" (Matthew 24:12 KJV). The Bible predicts in the last days there will be much hedonism (pursuit of pleasure as the highest good) and relativism (everyone makes their own "truth" for themselves).

3. Increase in false prophets.

The apostle Peter warned against false teachers in the end times (1 Peter 2:1; see also Jude 17-18). The Bible warns that in the end times people would forsake salvation in Christ for various types of occultism. Demonically inspired false religions would proliferate (see also Matthew 24:5; Mark 13:6).

4. The land of Israel.

"I will bring you from the nations...where you have been scattered" (Ezekiel 20:34 NIV; see also 37:1-14). Though the Jewish people were

without a homeland for 1,878 years, Isaiah 43:5-6 says that in the last days, *"I will bring your children from the ends of the earth."*

5. Conflict in the Middle East.

In the end times there will be *"wars and rumors of wars"* (Matthew 24:6-7). Ezekiel 38:1-6 predicts an invasion of Israel in the last days. Though written around 597 BC, the prophet Ezekiel assumes that Israel is in their land when armies attack in the "latter days."

6. The increasingly godless world system.

The final book of the New Testament, Revelation, depicts a coming era in which many facets of society will be organized around a centralized, unified entity. There will be a one-world economy (13:16-17), a one-world government (13:8; 17:1-18), and a one-world religion (13:8-12).

7. Increase of apostasy within the church.

Pastors often point out problems in the world; let me also admit that there are pockets of sin embedded within the ranks of the church. One of the signs of the end times relates to a Greek word that means, "rebellion" and "revolt." It is the word "apostasy," and its meaning is somewhat akin to the word "riot"—a free for all.

The Bible says that near the end of history many preachers will not preach the Scriptures, but will instead preach lies. They will speak pleasant words people want to hear and not the truth that will convert their souls. Having spent my life in all types of church work, let me say, we are in an era of serious theological apostasy (1 Timothy 4:1-2; 2 Timothy 4:3-4; 2 Thessalonians 2:3).

8. The wiring of the planet.

The book of Revelation describes several scenarios that people of previous generations found hard to believe. In fact, skeptics used to scoff at the idea that there could be a one-world money system, apart from which no one could buy or sell (Revelation 13:17). Skeptics mocked the idea that events happening in Israel could somehow be watched by the whole world at once (Revelation 11:3-12; 18:9-20).

We now live in a world of real-time video streaming, cyber currency, and digital footprints. We are constantly tracked via phones and other electronic cameras and devices, from Siri to Alexa, to personalized tracking of every purchase and online search. Along with the rise of influential leaders calling for socialism and global unification, the events in Revelation—fantastic as they may sound—are not only possible, but increasingly likely.

9. The rise of Islam.

The Bible predicted that the "children of Ishmael" would struggle against "the children of Isaac" throughout history (Genesis 16:12; 25:18). Aggression toward the Jews by Ishmael's descendants existed for centuries. But in AD 622, the founding of Islam would escalate this hostility immeasurably.

Past political leaders (such as Winston Churchill) and religious leaders (such as the Reformers) believed that near the end of history there would be an uprising of "Mohammedism." Much speculation has been raised about the 200 million soldiers predicted to assemble for the battle of Armageddon (Zechariah 14:1-4; Revelation 9:16-17). What worldview could summon that many followers of a warrior spirit who desire the extermination of both Jews *and* followers of Jesus? One theory suggests this army could include today's Muslims that oppose Israel. Even if this is not the case, the list of nations opposing Israel in the future described in Ezekiel 38 are predominantly Muslim, closely reflecting the attitudes of these nations toward Israel today.

10. A major outpouring of God's Holy Spirit, just prior to the rapture of the church.

The Scriptures speak of a great move of God before the final judgment of history (Joel 2:28-32; Zechariah 12:10-13:1). COVID-19 is prominent in the news, but spreading even faster than that life-threatening virus is the life-giving message of Christ. Surprisingly, the ranks of believers seem to grow fastest in the regions of intense persecution.

We may not see this as much in the U.S. and Europe, but in much of the world Christianity is growing exponentially. As the world battles COVID-19, it may ignite one more great revival of Christianity—and this may comprise the West's final visitation of the Holy Spirit, before Christ's return.

God has Called Us to Live Prepared

While spending that evening in the Jerusalem police station something occurred to me—the station was certainly in an interesting location. The

Garden Tomb of Jesus was only one street away, and the Golden Gate entry into Jerusalem's Old City was just across another street. I remember waiting in the lobby, noting that the main window was partially shattered as if a brick had once been thrown at it. And yet, only a few feet from that precinct office was the empty tomb of the One who once told the people, "Blessed are the peacemakers."

My group and I were frantically working to obtain new passports—our tickets "home." Jerusalem also is the city where purchase was made for another kind of passport. On a skull-shaped hill outside of Jerusalem, Jesus was crucified to purchase sufficient documentation into heaven for anyone who wants it. One Israeli official helped us get passports for home; yet another made it possible to get a passport for heaven.

"Is Jesus really coming back to earth? Literally? At any moment?" Let me say what I tell the people who have repeatedly asked me this in recent weeks: I absolutely believe the answer is, "Yes." Three decades of research, writing, and following world events convince me that this is true. But no one needs to be obsessively afraid regarding the end of time if they've accepted Christ's gracious offer of forgiveness before God.

Memes in a World Hungry for Meat

Most preachers today could be described as B-grade motivational speakers. Think about it—from the breakdown of the family, to unrestricted abortion, to Marxist BLM rioters descending on cities across America, to the June 2020 SCOTUS ruling classing transgender activity as an ethnicity—if there was ever a time for the pulpits of America to cry out for God's help and intervention, this would be that moment. Yet many church leaders remain silent.

In this land predicated on freedom of religious expression, July 2020 saw California churches warned that parishioners may no longer *sing* during worship services. And where was the unified, defiant cry from God's prophets and preachers, forcefully telling the Democrat-social-ist-pharaohs of our day to repent from their disregard of God, their undermining of liberty, and persecution of His church? It wasn't heard. Most pulpits today whimper forth with timid platitudes about "toler-ance" and "social justice," while few cut through sin's darkness to lead sinners toward Christ's light.

The Christian experience can't be adequately presented when reduced to memes and soundbites. As *Paradise Lost* author John Milton wrote in his poem of 1638, *Lycidas,* "The hungry sheep look up and are not fed." That's Christianity in 2020 America: The nation teeters on the brink of extinction, having reached this depth of lawlessness and sin—at least in part—because the church is more *polite* than *prophetic.* Conven-tional wisdom by expert "ministry strategists" over the past fifty years has coached generations of clergy more about how to be liked by people than approved by God. We look at the state of the home, the church, and the public square and have to ask, "How's that working for ya?"

Having spoken in more than 2,000 churches and having heard plenty of sermons, let me say that I passionately love the American church. I do. But it appears many of the 250,000-plus ordained ministers in America appear utterly impotent to preach in such a way as to begin igniting the spiritual awakening our country so desperately needs. When is the last time you heard a sermon calling lost sinners to flee from the eternal hell of which Scripture warns? When is the last time you have heard a minister speak on 1 Corinthians chapter 6, delineating various iniquities—moral offenses, sexual sins, including homosexuality—that if not repented of, will land their practitioners eternally outside of heaven? When?

When have you heard of ministers boldly organizing their cities to fast, pray for national awakening, and to beg God that churches and families be restored, and the Holy Spirit to subdue evil in this nation? Perhaps most of the exposure you've had to church services contained little more than milquetoast platitudes, cherry-picked servings of Bible-lite, and "God's helpful tips on how to become a better you!"

Dear friend, please know that the uncontrollable, all-powerful, living God of Scripture does care about you passionately—but He has so much more in store for you than merely being the "life coach" who is called on when needed. For America—and for you personally—Jesus Christ is offering rescue and restoration; but to do so, He must become Leader and Lord.

If you've spurned God, or if you think sin and eternity are a joke, then I humbly suggest you have more to fear than you could possibly realize. But to "whosoever will come," Jesus promised a peace beyond anything this world can offer. The One who is coming back to earth assures us, *"...Let not your heart be troubled, neither let it be afraid"* (John 14:27 NKJV).

2

NOT FOR SALE—OUR
MORAL COMPASS

n March of 2016, in my home state of North Carolina, House Bill 2 ("HB2—the bathroom bill" as it came to be known in the press) was signed into state law during the governorship of former Charlotte Mayor Pat McCrory. HB2 basically said public restrooms were to be used according to one's genetic sex; that is, men are to stay out of women's public restrooms, and vice versa. A tsunami of media attention descended on the state, and online condemnation of this "hateful" piece of legislation droned unrelenting. "How can people be so hateful toward those who identify as a gender different than from that of their birth?" The Twitterverse demanded to know.

North Carolina's HB2 was drafted in response to actual cases of voyeurs spying on women and girls in public restrooms and perverted men sneaking into retail changing rooms. The law was truly about the safety and privacy of people. But "woke" companies like PayPal and ESPN very publicly announced they would no longer conduct business with the state of North Carolina. Entertainers like Bruce Springsteen, Justin Bieber, and Taylor Swift—in righteous indignation against the transphobic state of North Carolina, proudly Tweeted their decisions not to perform in my home state. (Regarding Bieber deciding against holding a concert in the Tarheel state, I'd say we dodged a bullet there.)

But in endless op-eds condemning Governor McCrory's "reckless" support of HB2, the argument repeatedly cited regarding why it was bad policy to insist people only use the public facility of their own gender was *money*. As a student of American history and teacher of philosophy, I applauded HB2 because it affirmed what our Founders would have called natural law. But opponents of our infamous "bathroom bill" lamented the fact that HB2 had the potential to cause the state to lose business. The implied question became, "If acting morally results in the loss of money, isn't it better to act immorally and not lose money?" Be careful before answering "yes" to this question; Al Capone, John Gotti, and leaders of drug cartels would answer the same as today's progressives.

I am spending an inordinately long amount of space to talk about North Carolina's 2016 gubernatorial election for a purpose: I believe it constitutes a classic example of the good that might have been realized had citizens with sharp ethical sensibilities acted on the seriousness of the moment. For months leading up to the election, overtures were made to hundreds of very reluctant clergy throughout North Carolina, pleading with them to inform their congregations about the ways HB2 was being leveraged as a political tool to further ingrain moral relativism into the culture.

Despite targeted efforts by Tony Perkins (Family Research Council), James Dobson (Family Talk), Franklin Graham (Samaritan's Purse), Tim Wildmon (American Family Association), myself (Truth For A New Generation), and many others, McCrory would ultimately lose a governor's race watched by the whole nation. Over the past 25 years I have preached in all but about 10 of North Carolina's 100 counties. Voter drives and pastoral engagement meetings were held by conservatives in every single county. I personally spoke with more than 100 pastors in many of the state's largest churches, virtually all of which I had spoken in at one time or another. But one after another, clergy told me (and others) that they, "Just couldn't risk offending parishioners by weighing in on a 'peripheral' issue like HB2."

On election night, McCrory lost by less than 11,000 votes. Democratic victor Roy Cooper had run TV ads promising that if he were elected, there would be, "...no more silly moral legislation." In the state that saw (in 1587) the birth of the first English child on the North American continent, in this first colony to announce its autonomy and resolve independence from Great Britain (May, 1775; more than a year before the Declaration of Independence), in the state where the Battle of Guilford Courthouse (1781) inflicted enough damage on British troops that they would soon surrender at Yorktown, the highest elected official deemed morals as "silly."

It is hard to know what Jefferson—who held that moral law was "self-evident," "undeniable," and tied to the nature of God—would have thought. The Founders of 1776 laid everything on the line to birth a new nation, pledging, "...our lives, our fortunes, our sacred honor," and knew that they may likely die defending what they referred to as the moral cause of liberty. The men who steeled themselves by, "appealing to God for the rectitude of (their) intentions," could scarce have known that one day their descendants would dismiss moral truth as irrelevant. The eighteenth century's pulpits throughout the 13 colonies ignited the revolution for America's liberties. Almost no pulpits in the twenty-first century could be roused to defend them.

Money Over Morals:
When Sacred Becomes "Silly"

Predictably, three months into his tenure as governor, Roy Cooper kept his campaign promise and repealed House Bill 2. Progressive advocacy groups hailed this as a "courageous" step for human rights. But Cooper's short-sighted denials of natural law, moral truth, freedom of religion, and human biology in general result in the following: people (especially children) are again unprotected from opportunistic perverts lurking and watching around public restrooms, locker rooms, and changing rooms. Guarding that legacy of protecting sexual predators puts women and children at risk. Second, Cooper set yet another forensic precedent of obstructing government based on natural law. Trans-rights (like gay rights and abortion rights) are not universally recognized, intuitively understood, immutable natural rights. They are manufactured rights.

Eventually, one of these two will have to give: Either the growing list of assumed/manufactured rights (recognized, codified, and demanded over the course of the last several decades) will have to fall, or the U.S. Constitution, which assumed the validity of undeniable moral truths recognized throughout all of history, will have to fall.

Think about it—is it so radical to say that in public areas where privacy could be compromised, that biological males are restricted to changing rooms or restrooms for males, and females must only use restrooms and changing rooms for females? For the progressives of the twenty-first century, objectively defining "men as men" and "women as women" is, indeed, too radical.

Celebrities, sports figures, and pundits from every medium weighed in on North Carolina's "backward" legislation. Clearly, the Internet opined, these backward southerners were fearful of anyone who is "different." Sophisticated, urbane, woke advocates needed to help prejudiced North Carolinian "haters" realize a binary view of gender is so last century. A new lexicon of terminology began to emerge in the quest for justice for transgenders: cisgender (from the Latin word for "same"). If you were born a genetic male and you live as, dress as, and identify as a male, you are cisgender. (And I've read more than a few blogs that sarcastically call cis's "dull" and "unimaginative.")

The topic of transgenderism as a political cause has confronted me in countless media interviews over the past several years. The HB2 "bathroom bill" in North Carolina brought the larger subject of gender dysphoria to the nation's front page. During panel discussions at universities, I have been taken to task by pro-trans students who would come to the mic and object to my binary (read, "biased," "myopic," "phobic") view of gender. Sometimes, vocally so.

Speaking at a college shortly before the quarantine, I was in respectful dialogue with a young man who insisted he was actually female. A couple of audience members spoke in the individual's defense, saying to me, "You can't label *him*!" And, "*She* doesn't have to acquiesce to anybody's labels! Society doesn't have the right to define *her*...." When I teach students critical thinking skills and how to spot fallacies in the course of public dialogue, I call such assumed conclusions, "refusal to debate." Counter-facts are set forth as true— *no discussion allowed.*

> As more politically-correct, progressive "truths" are set before us in the media, an unsuspecting public is made to think that lies are facts through the tactic of "refusal to debate."

The individual being discussed by others quietly stood there amid the growing gale of debate about gender. His poorly applied makeup was barely able to hide the facial shadow of emerging whiskers that looked to be about 24 hours past needing to be shaved. I realized that being in a position to move people toward agreeing with and fighting for something clearly counter to reality is, among other things, about power.

Though they may not say it publicly, every credentialed mental health professional in America knows that the humane treatment of someone confused about their gender is counseling, not surgery. Every scientist and medical doctor knows that male and female genders are objective conditions. We all possess either a XX or XY chromosomal makeup and this is not merely an oppressive social construct. But faculty and students enrolled in American colleges today are unable to ascertain what others see as undeniable truths.

Regarding women who identify as women, the discussion turned to one of the physiological realities of womanhood, menstruation. I brought up this formerly delicate subject in an attempt to clarify what "female-ness" actually is—because it is so difficult to grasp, apparently. Speaking as politely as I could with the trans college student, I requested permission to ask a personal question. He/she said it would be okay for me to do so, and I gently asked the transgendered student if he (she) had begun menstruating. There was silence for what seemed like a long time. The student looked up and offered, "That is not a part of my experience as a female."

"Don't just assume he's a mennie..." a very "woke" nearby student sneered. I later learned that "mennie" is a derogatory term used by pro-transgender activists describing several things: Genetic females who identify as women (thus, cisgenders), and who menstruate;

Genetic females who identify as men (thus, transgender male), but who menstruate; Finally, any narrow, biased, anti-gender-fluidity people (trans-phobics) who assume that having a period is something only women do. Confused yet?

What Our Abandonment of Morality Means Long-Term

My heart felt great compassion for that male student and others like him, groping in search of their place in this world. It is only natural to seek a stable sense of self. We all want to feel that we have found our place and fit in. Sadly, these quests are leading many down countless paths of deviancy. Many today are throwing themselves into homosexuality and transgenderism, and though they now have legal and cultural support for their fantasy pursuits, such Millennials and younger are finding themselves empty.

Years ago, I used to say that the most closely guarded value of this country was sexual license. Now I say that the core value of the nation is simply, license—the ability to do anything I want, and to not answer to anybody. There has been a cry for a sort of "militant autonomy." Our nation, and courts, have bowed to it; and yet, people are still searching. We are a nation of opulence and indulgence, a country of personal prosperity and prerogative—so why are we unhappy?

America is now more than four decades into our journey of abandonment of beliefs concerning objective morality. The Civil Rights Act of 1964 was predicated on the fact that objective moral truths exist—that all humans are equal in worth, value, dignity, and personhood. Only seven years later, in 1973, our SCOTUS caved to the abortion lobby and adjudicated that one person's claim to a manufactured right (privacy, in regard to terminating a pregnancy) superseded another person's experience of a natural right—life.

Emma Lazarus' sonnet, written on lady Liberty's famed pedestal, promises sanctuary for the, "...tired, poor, huddled masses yearning to breathe free." The promise of American liberty should not, however, be interpreted to guarantee affirmation (and coddling) for the deluded, malicious, deviant, or insurrectional, yearning to be validated. The loss of our moral compass endangers the preservation of our Constitution. Third U.S. President James Madison said it—only for a moral and religious people will this American experiment work. This is part of why it is in the best interest of all people to speak up for—and by voting, stand up—for morality.

Stand up for moral truth and you're helping to stand up for the preservation of America. Those who love God and country aren't being hateful toward anyone and we're certainly not phobic or afraid. Shame us, flame us, unfriend us if you must, but it is time for moral courage.

But like Abraham, Moses, Aristotle, Augustine, Aquinas, Shakespeare, Lincoln, both Roosevelts, the Wright brothers, C.S. Lewis, Churchill, Dr. King, Mother Teresa, Reagan, Billy Graham, and a host of other notables (and not to leave out a certain Jesus of Nazareth), we acknowledge that some things are absolutely right, and some things are absolutely wrong.

And unless we quickly summon the courage to fight the false and defend the true, we'll be absolutely beyond the point of no return. And that is a fact.

3

WHAT THE LEFT HAS PLANNED FOR AMERICA—AND WHY

"Of all tyrannies, a tyranny sincerely exercised for the good of its victims may be the most oppressive. It would be better to live under robber barons than under omnipotent moral busybodies. The robber baron's cruelty may sometimes sleep, his cupidity may at some point be satiated; but those who torment us for our own good will torment us without end, for they do so with the approval of their own conscience." —**C.S. Lewis,** *God in the Dock: Essays on Theology*

Life is full of little reminders that we need to be right with God. Life's circumstances throw you some pretty big reminders, too. A baby's gentle giggle or the sight of a beautiful sunset each moves us inside, reminding us of the artistry of God exhibited throughout His creation. Getting a speeding ticket while in a school zone or the embarrassment of being caught in a lie—these would cast a sense of heavy conviction over most people, leading to some soul-searching and mending of one's ways. Things like a cancer diagnosis or the untimely death of someone close to us cause the wise to ponder eternity and consider where they stand with God.

With varying degrees of gentleness and sometimes force, the Lord "elbows" through life's events in order to get our attention. Theologian C.S. Lewis said that God whispers to us through our pleasures, speaks to us in day-to-day life, but shouts at us in the deep valley of pain: "Pain is God's megaphone to rouse a deaf world," said the famed scholar. Holocaust survivor Corrie Ten Boom wisely noted, "When life knocks you to your knees, well, that's a pretty good place to pray, isn't it?"

Let me tell you about a perennial circumstance of life that makes me think about God in a big way: The DMV. I am completely serious. Spend a day going back and forth to the Department of Motor Vehicles, desperately trying to get your license plate issues sorted out before they flip the "CLOSED" sign around at 4:59 p.m., and you'll do some hard praying, I assure you. About the third time you stand in line for 45 minutes and get sent back to the bank across town because the notary left off a comma that was supposed go between their signature and the date, you'll be crying out for divine intervention. On a recent trip to the DMV, I watched a man argue with the attendant over some technicality, and let's just say the irate customer loudly discussed heaven and hell in non-theological terms. It was awkward.

So, if going to the DMV has been as frustrating and counterproductive as it so often is for many people, imagine if the entire country was run that way. But the legendary inefficiencies characteristic of a trip to the DMV appear almost *endearing* when compared to the sinister—and dangerous—America promised in the events of 2020.

"Woe to those who call evil good and good evil, who substitute darkness for light and light for darkness..." (Isaiah 5:20 NASB).

More than six weeks' of news coverage showing the burning of downtown districts in cities like Dallas, Seattle, Portland, Minneapolis—and probably towns large and small near you—is part of why many dub 2020, "The year from hell." While George Floyd's death at the hands of murderous cop Derek Chauvin on May 25, 2020, truly was an inexcusable homicide, the vandalism and lawlessness that followed is equally wrong. We have heard much about protecting the civil rights of minorities from abusive law enforcement, and rightly so, but who is speaking up for the civil rights of innocent citizens and business owners when paid protestors bring their bricks to town to throw in your windows? Rioters are being given access to funding, infrastructure, organizational know-how, and have *definitely* been given a freepass on social distancing compliance.

> "Narrowing the boundaries of what can be said without fear of reprisal..."

"We uphold the value of robust and even caustic counter-speech from all quarters. But it is now all too common to hear calls for swift and severe retribution in response to perceived transgressions of speech and thought." This statement is from a letter published in *Harper's* magazine and online, July 7, 2020, and signed by 30 politically liberal public figures, all of whom warn against the severely intolerant culture of the "socially woke" left.

In a type of treason that would have been unimaginable to America's Founders, progressive liberals are pleased with the anarchy, burned buildings, and street violence George Floyd's apparent murder initiated. But much more than store windows have been shattered: public peace, the rule of law, and national stability all lie in ruins, too. And the Democrats are glad. *Thrilled,* would be a more accurate description.

> *"Do not follow the crowd in doing wrong"* (Exodus 23:2 NIV).

Why? Why would any rational person who cares about America be *glad* about the civil unrest and tangible losses incurred by their fellow citizens? To understand liberal / progressive persons in power and those who aspire to be, from the previous sentence you must take out the words "rational" and the part about "caring for America."

If you discovered roaches in your kitchen, you wouldn't solve the problem by burning down the house. You'd be rid of the roaches, but you'd have nowhere to stay. That would be an example of the old maxim, "Don't swat a fly with a sledgehammer." It is just not rational.

But if you're trying to understand the left's rationale for violence, desecration of public monuments, and anarchy in public buildings in the aftermath of George Floyd's tragic murder, you must come to grips with the reality that *this disorder is a tactic of the socialists to attempt to usher in new order.* Believe me—my natural inclination to always assume the best about people kept me from this conclusion for a long time. But hardline progressives set the philosophy of the Democratic party right now; they have *owned* America's newsrooms and classrooms for several decades. (To learn more about the ideological wars in the realms of journalism and education, please carefully study titles in the Recommended Reading list in Appendix C).

If the Democrats prevail in the 2020 elections, three realms will turn "hard left" and the United States will become irrevocably socialist before the next 4-year term is over. I am absolutely convinced that within ten years or less, the U.S. Constitution will be substantially rewritten, if not abolished completely. As a nation, we truly are at "the moment" of decision—the America that was built on moral truth and godly principles is about to drift beyond the point of restoration. Perhaps it already has.

Progressives are committed to change any laws necessary to see to it that they never lose control again of federal, state, and local governments. And ignorance of history is one of the tools in their toolkit. Keep upcoming generations uninformed about our nation's glorious past and even our nation's enviable *present*, in terms of quality of life compared to the rest of the world.

What will emanate from a White House and Congress led by the current wave of pro-socialist / progressives, should they win major races throughout the land? Given the mindset firmly adopted by Democrats of the 21st century, what "accomplishments" will they have in store for the American people? Consider the following; rumblings of any or all of these can be found in the news of the recent months.

Twenty One realities in America's future if the current rush toward liberal/progressivism isn't stopped:

1. In the next administration, add 2-4 justices to the Supreme Court, which they can easily do with a president, vice president, and fifty Democrat senators.

2. Give citizenship (including voting rights) to approximately 15 million illegals.

3. Relax border security, ultimately adding more between 1 and 2 million new "undocumented" voters to rolls each year.

4. Increase the number of legal immigrants annually allowed into the U.S.

5. Allow unregistered voters to show up, register, and vote all in one, on election days.

6. Mail-in ballots become the norm, and allowing people to "proxy vote" for others will become law.

7. In the name of "justice and civil rights, it will be outlawed to require a photo ID when voting.

8. Election days will become Federal holidays.

9. The Electoral College will be abolished.

10. The voting age will be reduced to 16 or 17 years of age, and students will be allowed to (encouraged to) vote in their high schools.

11. Former felons will be restored the right to vote (and possibly even inmates serving time) will be allowed to vote.

12. Repeal of the Hyde Amendment (currently prohibiting the use of tax dollars to pay for abortions) will take place soon after the inauguration of our next Democrat president.

13. Military spending will be greatly reduced.

14. The pressure to limit the authority of local law enforcement will intensify. Federal funding to states for roads and schools will be withheld, contingent on compliance with liberal policies coming out of Washington. Local citizens will have less and less say about their own municipalities, and about their security in general.

15. Private ownership of guns will become illegal.

16. Religious activities will be strictly restricted to the inside of churches, synagogues, and mosques.

17. Criticism of liberal beliefs and immoral behaviors will become "Hate Speech," punishable by fines and/or jail time.

18. Entitlements: Health care, a guaranteed income, and "free" college tuition will be given to all, citizen and non-citizen, whether or not they agree to work.

19. Billions of dollars will be spent for reparations, beginning first with disbursements to African Americans, then quickly to other "oppressed" ethnicities as well.

20. Green energy policies will continue to dominate the platforms of Democrat candidates and leaders. Mandate to comply with the minutiae of enviro-friendly laws will be enforced not only for businesses, but also upon homeowners.

21. American sovereignty will be relinquished to mandates coming forth from the United Nations and the World Health Organization. Though the full ceding of leadership may take as much as a decade, ultimately, leadership of America will be in the hands of committees staffed by representatives from member nations of the UN and WHO.

For those who value our morally based, Constitutional, representative republic;

For all who believe that, warts and all, this is still the greatest place to live in the world;

For all who know that our nation's founding and first two centuries were *not* the genocidal horror show the left claims it was;

For all who believe that patriotism is a good thing, and that love of one's country is something to be encouraged;

For all who understand that the U.S. has been and is unique and who don't apologize for what progressives disdain as, "American exceptionalism";

For all who still believe in praying for America, knowing there is a God in heaven who rules and reigns in the affairs of all people;

For all who believing that the discipline of getting up and going to work a job is not only an honorable thing, but is truly a privilege;

For all who know that the last thing to which our Founders would ever have consented would be the confiscation of one person's hard-earned wages to freely give others who wouldn't work;

And finally,

For all who, like the Founders, believe in the principle of "consent of the governed," and that it is wrong for the government to tax the citizens into poverty, and then to control those citizens' lives with no hope of dissent or reprisal...

...Then I ask, "Are you ready to vote, about now? Do you think God-fearing, freedom-loving Americans should do their utmost to pray, influence others, and vote?"

The attacks on America have been political, philosophical, cultural, but most of all, *spiritual*. This is why it is so vital for you to be involved. If America is to be *saved* we will need the prayers and involvement of the same things it took for America to be *birthed*—pervasive involvement and good citizenship by all, and throughout the land. As authors Robert Hutchins and Mortimer Adler challenged readers in *The Great Conversation* (stirring introduction to the "Great Books of the Western World" series, first released in 1952), "It is now necessary for all of us to live *at the height of our times*."

I urge you to get informed, stay informed, be willing to talk to your family members and neighbors regarding the state of the country. Vote and volunteer—be willing to invest time in your local precincts, and recruit others to do the same.

Most of all, I urge you to pray. We are in a battle for the survival of free America established under God's laws. Moral truth still matters, and the laws of God still stand. The Lord Jesus has not ceased to exist nor has His truth gone out of date. Get involved, stay involved, because we are in a battle.

4

MAKE YOUR
VOICE HEARD

The riots in Minneapolis and the spread of violence across the nation in the aftermath of the senseless death of George Floyd has escalated racial issues to the forefront of American discussion. What's the answer? How can we make a difference in a world where many people are taking out their frustrations in destructive and deadly ways?

I am sure that, like myself, your heart was hurt to see the coverage of the riots that began in Minneapolis and coalesced into violence in cities throughout America. The senseless murder of George Floyd by rogue officer Derek Chauvin has been the catalyst for hundreds of protests, and sadly, much violence, looting, uprisings against authorities, and even several deaths and murders.

From the president, to governors and mayors, to influential celebrities—many people pled with protesters to rein in the anger and destruction. NBA Hall of Famer Michael Jordan released a statement that resonates with what many are saying, that people understand the hurt oppressed minorities have had, but also desire for the violence to end.

As we look at the push for civil rights in America, now and in times past, we all want the noble aspirations of our Declaration of Independence to be realized in the U.S.: "...that all [people] are created equal, that they are endowed by their Creator with certain inalienable Rights, that among these are Life, Liberty and the pursuit of Happiness." How we all wish before God that these truths were our current reality.

Being made in the image of God, the *imago Dei*, clearly shows all people possess equal worth, value, and dignity. Jefferson wrote the profound words in the Declaration, master calligrapher Timothy Matlack wrote the beautiful wording, and John Hancock was the first of 56 delegates to sign. To this day, people speak of "Signing your John Hancock" when writing one's name in a vivid way. John Hancock wanted the King of England to unmistakably see that he and the other signers were not afraid to declare their independence.

Jefferson's words of "all men created equal" have been and are true to this day. But as we realize, because this is a world of sin and imperfect individuals, people are often abused, exploited, oppressed, and violated. This is tragic, and unjust. But the way to fight injustice is not with injustice. The way to fight evil is not with more darkness.

I was shocked to read in the news over the weekend that some liberal activists are using money to pay bail for some of the most violent felons in the riots. The same liberals who unwaveringly enforce the quarantines and who fervently stand against allowing normal citizens to resume their jobs and activities, are among the same pro-lockdown liberals working to allow rioters to evade justice.

Why would some people in our nation seem to have a vested interest in major cities being in a state of lawlessness? Straight from the playbooks of socialists from Karl Marx to Saul Alinsky, a society in a state of upheaval, constant civil unrest, danger, economic stagnation, and growing lawlessness, leads to such a state of disorder it becomes possible to introduce new order.

We all want every person's constitutionally protected natural rights to be experienced. No one's moral rights or natural rights should be undermined. And certainly no one's life should be stolen away from them, as George Floyd's was.

But our stand against murder and injustice must not be expressed through crime and mass disorder. We are not saving the country by weakening the country. Let's look at leaders from the past who blazed the trail of civil rights leadership for the rest of us. The name of the organization led by Dr. Martin Luther King Jr. was the Southern Christian Leadership Coalition. To march with Dr. King, a person had to pass several levels of scrutiny. Fellow protesters were "vetted out," and here are just a few of the points of agreement, including nonviolence, that a marcher had to sign his name to with a witness. The following list is from King's book *Why We Can't Wait:*

1. Meditate daily on the teachings and life of Jesus.

2. Remember always that the nonviolent movement in Birmingham seeks justice and reconciliation—not victory.

3. Walk and talk in the manner of love, for God is love.

4. Pray daily to be used by God in order that all men might be free.

5. Sacrifice personal wishes in order that all men might be free.

6. Observe with both friend and foe the ordinary rules of courtesy.

7. Seek to perform regular service for others and for the world.

8. Refrain from the violence of fist, tongue, or heart.

9. Strive to be in good spiritual and bodily health.

10. Follow the directions of the movement and of the captain on a demonstration.[6]

In doing research for the seventeen books I have written, and hundreds of published articles, it has been my honor to interview many people, including several who marched with Dr. King in the 1960s. I have interviewed his niece a half dozen times, Dr. Alveda King, and she has spoken for us at our Truth For A New Generation conferences. Dr. Alveda King was with her uncle throughout the civil rights movement and was even there the Sunday afternoon that plans for the civil rights movement were first discussed in Dr. King's living room.

Dr. Alveda King and others who knew him agree that Martin Luther King Jr. would be heartbroken at the violence and rioting of today. He would have never embraced lawlessness in a quest to somehow bring forth justice and righteousness.

Another name that we would do well to hear from is Rev. Francis J. Grimke (1850-1937). Grimke was a Presbyterian minister, former slave, and early child civil rights leader. Decades before Dr. King, Rev. Grimke said, "The secession of the Southern States in 1860 was a small matter compared with the secession of the Union itself from the great principles enunciated in the Declaration of Independence, in the Golden Rule, in the Ten Commandments, (and) in the Sermon on the Mount. Unless we hold—and hold firmly—to these great fundamental principles of righteousness, our Union...will be 'only a covenant with death, and an agreement with hell.'"[7]

Abraham Lincoln, during the hardest days of his presidency, and in his fight to reverse Dredd Scott, legislate emancipation, and preserve the United States, said, "I have been driven many times to my knees by the overwhelming conviction that I had absolutely no other place to go."[8]

Here are the voices that must ring out, to the saving of our nation:

1. Your voice: in prayer. Please intercede for this country!

2. The "voice" of citizens voting. I urge you to both pray and vote your values, seeking leaders who will govern in ways that square with our Constitution as written, and with God's truth as written on our hearts.

3. We need to hear the voices of godly leaders—those in position of influence who will call their fellow citizens to moral truth, God, family, and moral actions.

There is another voice this nation needs to hear. This is a voice I need to hear, and perhaps right now, even today, *you* need to hear, from the One Scripture describes as having a "still, small voice...." Our nation needs to hear from God. We need the Holy Spirit of God to work in our nation today. May the Lord break through the noise of our times, speak to every person in one accord (and remember, God is not the author of disorder), and let us hear Him say as in Isaiah 30:21 (KJV), "...*This is the way, walk ye in it....*"

How to Use Your Voice for Good

It has become an infamous statistic: 81 percent of white evangelicals voted for Donald J. Trump in 2016.[9] But that is only part of the story.

The same Pew Research study that released this information also noted the following:

- 52 percent of Catholics voted for Trump, up from 48 percent for Romney in 2012.
- 61 percent of Mormons voted for Trump.
- 29 percent of "other faiths" voted for Trump, an increase of 12 percent from 2012.
- 26 percent of Hispanic Catholics voted for Trump, an increase of 8 percent from 2012.

President Trump not only earned the clear majority of white evangelical votes, but the votes of the majority of Mormons (who are also generally pro-life and support religious liberty) and received an unexpected larger share of votes among those of "other faiths," perhaps including minority religious groups who saw Trump as offering greater religious freedoms. Though still only receiving a small percentage of Hispanic Catholic votes, Trump's pro-life position likely influenced his gain among this voting segment.

The one other overlooked factor in Trump's surprise presidential win can be found in the number of overall voters in 2016—60.2 percent of the voting-eligible population voted in 2016, an increase over the 58.6 percent in 2012, though lower than 2008.[10] Though only a difference of 2 percent, this segment may have made the difference in the election. More people voted their values in 2016 than in the previous election, particularly in certain battleground states, an outcome that did not come by accident.

Both sides pushed for voter registration and "getting out the vote," yet Trump supporters somehow motivated more people to vote than in the past. This involved many Americans leveraging connections to get more voters involved. One commentator noted:

> In a sense, the choice isn't surprising. Trump's nominee to the Supreme Court, Neil Gorsuch, is unambiguously pro-life, and Trump's promise to "destroy" the Johnson Amendment—a provision in the tax code barring non-profits from political participation—closely follows the evangelical playbook.
>
> But in another way, Christian support for Trump is puzzling. Trump's Christian bona fides are (at best) shaky and his personal demeanor, marked by swashbuckling moral indecency, contradicts the evangelical temperament. Evangelicals made these concerns widely known during the campaign. *The Atlantic* noted how the Trump vote "concealed deep, painful fractures."
>
> Still, for all the angst over electing a moral reprobate, the evangelicals delivered. Why? One explanation is pragmatic: The ends (desired political outcomes) justified the means (Trump's ethically offensive personal demeanor).[11]

From this writer's perspective, voters overlooked Trump's weaknesses as a person to vote for his policies—religious freedom/conservative and American values.

As others have noted, part of Trump's victory is less based on what he offered America as what Hillary Clinton offered America. How many voted "against Clinton" rather than "for Trump" may never be fully known, but the convergence of a clear progressive offering four to eight more years of Obama policy versus a voice offering a return to make America great again was enough to settle their conscience.

A look at this roller coaster election offers some valuable insights into both the importance and the methods of leveraging connections for change in our nation. Trump's campaign focused on connecting with as many people as possible, connecting on as many issues as possible (though not every issue), and connecting with the emotions of those who could support his cause.

Connecting With as Many People as Possible

Just as Obama's celebrity connections and mass events in 2008 helped support his road to the White House, Donald Trump utilized the concept of connecting with as many people as possible to his advantage during his campaign. In August 2015, the public first began to catch a glimpse of the popularity of Trump as a candidate. While many Republican contenders scrambled for media attention and crowds, Trump's Alabama event, originally scheduled for a 4,300-seat venue, was changed to a stadium with a 40,000-plus person capacity. According to the left-leaning CNN report of the event, 30,000 turned out for the rally.[12]

Perhaps what made this event more surprising was not the number of people involved, but the location—Mobile, Alabama. Events this size almost only happen for college football, not for politicians. Trump had connected with the hearts of America's heartland in a way other Republican candidates had not. The event became somewhat of a turning point, providing him with a stronger advantage over other frontrunners of the time, such as Ted Cruz and Marco Rubio, while speaking out against Jeb Bush during his speech.

Later rallies continued to increase Trump's widespread connections with the American public. Though some were unsurprised at his acceptance in the South, his appearance to 14,000 people in Columbus, Ohio, a key battleground state, on November 23, 2015, caused a growing concern for Clinton's campaign. His appearance to approximately 10,000 people in February 2016 in Tampa, Florida, also showed his strength, both among his Republican primary rivals and his fight against Hillary Clinton.

Connecting on as Many Issues as Possible

During his campaign, Trump made numerous promises, emphasizing America first. As the election drew closer, he began to more clearly outline his areas of commitment, such as his promises to appoint conservative Supreme Court justices, protect America's borders, and grow American jobs, among others.

One year into his presidency, *USA Today* noted a list of Trump's accomplishments, citing:[13]

- **Judicial appointments**: Neil Gorsuch, as well as 12 justices on the U.S. Court of Appeals.
- **Anti-abortion actions**: Expanding a 1984 prohibition of U.S. aid to international groups supporting abortion.
- **Elevating religious protections**: Including the signing of a new executive order protecting religious liberties.

- **Weighing in on Supreme Court cases**: Such as Jack Phillip's Colorado cake baker case.

- **Recognizing Jerusalem as capital of Israel**: A major shift from the previous administration.

- **Allowing federal money to pay to rebuild churches**: FEMA can now allow churches to receive federal dollars to rebuild after natural disasters.

- **Directing aid to persecuted Christians through faith-based groups**: The State Department can now bypass the UN to directly help religious minorities persecuted in Iraq.

- **Doubling the tax credit for children**: Part of Trump's first-year tax reform, this represented one tangible way to give American families a bit of financial relief.

These issues that helped pave the way for Trump's election also stand key to his reelection. Though much work remains, the administration's fulfillment of policies on important issues points toward what may be a landslide victory for Trump-Pence in 2020.

While we are not running a presidential campaign, our efforts to lead change touch on certain issues we can use as rallying points. For example, in my work leading Truth For A New Generation, I emphasize the need to teach young people a biblical worldview. Why? If recent studies show only 4 percent of American teenagers have a biblical worldview, what will that lead to for the future of America? How will this impact education, government, and family? What will this lead to for the future of the pro-life movement? How will our churches look in 20 years as a result, as well as our nation?

Whatever your key issue, it likely holds consequences for a variety of other topics. For Trump, making America great again related to numerous positions critical to the success of his presidential campaign. When I served with Focus on the Family years ago with Dr. James Dobson, the focus was built right into the name of the organization. Dr. Dobson clearly represented a name devoted to helping families. His work led to one of the largest Christian family organizations in America's history, influencing both the local neighbor's house and the White House.

Connecting With the Emotions of Those Who Can Help

Trump has never been known as a quiet guy. In his presidential campaign, he clearly and boldly used emotion to connect with those angry with America's direction. He emphasized patriotism, religious freedom, job growth, and most important to his efforts, making America great again. A certain nostalgia connected to this simple phrase drew in veterans, working-class families, religious conservatives, as well as many who had remained at home during the previous election—all because Trump connected with their emotions.

Of top importance to me and to my work was his focus on religious liberties. The supposed wall between church and state continues to stand as a key point of debate between many in this nation. In April 2017, a Freedom From Religion Foundation (FFRF) supported a dozen new billboards throughout the Denver area that claimed, "The only wall we need is between church and state."

The group also claimed the billboards were timely because of the then impending confirmation of Supreme Court nominee Neil Gorsuch, whom FFRF calls a "threat to secular government and individual liberties, given his 'natural law' philosophy derived from religious principles." An FFRF Denver chapter leader also said, "At no time in the history of the United States have our First Amendment rights possibly been more threatened than they are today."

I couldn't agree more—but for much different reasons: The argument many have about the separation between church and state is *grossly* misconstrued. Our Founders never intended that faith be stripped from the public square. In fact, in their zeal to remove all references of religion, many of these "freedom from faith" organizations would have to take our founding fathers to court, too.

At that time, I debated the leader of an organization similar to FFRF, Michael L. "Mikey" Weinstein, founder and president of the Military Religious Freedom Foundation (MRFF), for a live evening debate. Held at Colorado Christian University, we discussed the views of America's early leaders and implications for today. Though a strong representative of his view, the emotions of many in the audience resonated more with the idea of religious freedom represented by a true and historically accurate presentation of the separation of church and state.

The Connection Hillary Never Made

In September 2016, I listened to the presidential debate between Hillary Clinton and Donald Trump. I cringed as Hillary threw out one reductionist fallacy after another on any number of issues—especially regarding her gross mischaracterizations of business, the lot of American workers, and how the economy supposedly works.

Within the first five minutes of the debate, Hillary piously intoned, "We need an economy that works for everyone, not just for those at the top." Think about that jab at "those at the top"—from someone whose husband is paid more per speech than most people *make in a year*. It was another sickening dose of "faux solidarity with the little guy" from a woman whose corrupt Clinton Foundation amassed a *quarter of a billion dollars in cash* while she was serving as secretary of state. Talk about conflicts of interest, duplicity in words and actions, and the making of money off the backs of the American people.

Hillary quickly brought out the leftist promise to raise the minimum wage to $15 per hour—the net effect of which would further tether prime-of-life adults to entry-level jobs, not really creating sustainable "careers." But Clinton also promised that companies would be required to engage in profit-sharing with employees. Even Barack Obama, on his most Marxist, anti-free-market economy day, never hinted at that. Two speakers on the stage: which one was the friend to workers?

Such talk plays well with frustrated people at the lower end of the earning spectrum who are convinced that the "system" has limited their options. Democrats get a lot of mileage in making blanket promises of greater income, topped with a mentality that implies that "together, we can stick it to the man." And for those who have never owned a business of any size, never had to make sure employees get paid every two weeks, and who are confused about where wealth comes from, Democrat criticisms of profit and American business sound appropriate.

From Shakespeare to Jane Austin to Charles Dickens (and even in the Bible's depiction of Mary Magdalene) literature has come back time and again to ponder the image of "the fallen woman." And much like a once-idealistic woman, now indigent, out of options and out of ideas, the Democratic party is prostituting themselves for votes. Ministering in Amsterdam in the year 2000, I watched the prostitute/addicts reach out needle-riddled arms to tourists, shouting, "Ten guilders, five guilders... ok, ok, one guilder, to do anything you want!" (This was before the Netherlands switched to the euro in 2002.)

No Amsterdam harlot works their street any more diligently than the Democrats are now working the American electorate. Having made a step toward eventual communism, Democrats such as Alexandria Ocasio-Cortez, Rashida Tlaib, Ilhan Omar, Kamala Harris, and Elizabeth Warren (like the Clintons before them) now sell platitudes to the masses and national security to international Muslim leaders. For votes, dollars, or special-interest influence, we could say that the socialism-promoting Democrats are selling their party and its platform. But what they are really doing is selling out America, like a prostitute selling her body for the very drugs that will finish killing it. Socialist politics—like drug addiction or harlotry—is a toxic life to a quick death. So, why do the Democrats appear *absolutely committed* to take us there?

While I am convinced that in 2016 Hillary Clinton knew her scripts amounted to one diabolical lie, it is clear that as a candidate she was deeply wedded to this philosophy. After all, everyone's soul is ultimately loyal to something. But heaven forbid that the "land of the free" irrevocably sell its soul to the doctrines of Marxism. Spiritually, socially, economically, politically—hers is a brand from which we would not recover.

Here's how jobs and wealth are created: through ingenuity, hard work, and risk. Contrary to Hillary's sales pitch to the masses, small business growth doesn't involve the exploitation of anyone. For example, my friend Arnold took his retirement nest egg of $200,000 and built a business around an idea he had for harvesting sod grass. Putting his own capital at risk, he and his wife began working some of the longest days of their lives at a time in which most of their peers would have been taking things easy.

Putting everything into this new venture, they even lived out of a warehouse for over a year, working late, believing in their idea and themselves. And when they eventually sold the enterprise they had carefully nurtured; the valuation of the sod business was over $2 million. As they retired a second time, their hard work and risk not only provided them with a sizable return, but 14 people now had jobs. A new owner had a sustainable company to run and grow.

But for every story like this (and there are hundreds), the success stories of countless other Americans will never be told because they will never happen. That's because any shred of faith in themselves or belief in America was crushed by a suffocating message like the one intoned by Hillary during her debate. The creativity and personal actualization of millions is squelched by the toxic philosophy of the left. Their voter base dare not be told that there is a way of escape (as in the growing #WalkAway movement).

In contrast, that night Donald Trump (the candidate, and throughout his presidency) has continued to present his overarching message of making America great again. It was not eloquent, but it was emotional—and it worked.

The conservative message (like America, and life itself, really) is simple. Say your prayers, work hard, do the right thing, and play by the rules. At the end of the day, God (not government) will "have your back," and you'll know that your own character and sweat kept the lights on and put food on the table. There's no fall into an emotional black hole of blaming some elusive boogeyman for life's struggles.

Trump, for all his inelegant bluster, understands the liberating joy of self-reliance. Hillary, who repeats carefully scripted fiction with machine-like precision, needs the masses to need her. Such pathology is not how great nations of liberty and creativity are built. Abusive relationships and cults, maybe, but not thriving nations of prosperous people. The American people made their choice, ushering in a new era of political leadership.

What It's All About

Let me boil this discussion down to one proposition. In the first scenario with the election of Trump, the judgment of God may have been stayed because we as a nation are beginning to repent of our embrace of death and darkness. And by this, I mean that the American people have voted to turn away from the abortion industry and the legislation of immorality imposed by judicial fiat.

In the second scenario, if Hillary Clinton had been voted president, I'm firmly convinced that the judgment of God on America would have intensified, because we would have voted to maintain and even enhance our genocide of infants and our societal lawlessness. Much like the choices God gave Israel in Deuteronomy 30:19, America was choosing between life and death.

Perhaps, laying a foundation of life and grace for generations of Americans not yet born, God has favored us with leaders who revere Him and believe in moral truth. Let us hope so.

But regardless of what tomorrow brings, the priorities of life for the Christian citizen remain unchanged—we are to love God and grow in Christ. We are to grow in grace, love our neighbor, and daily live as citizens of two kingdoms. As St. Augustine noted, Christ's followers walk in two worlds: the city of God and the city of mankind, with responsibility to both. Pity the people who live under leaders who only recognize existence of the latter. Pity more the people blind enough, selfish enough, and greedy enough to repeatedly elect such.

I believe that leaders of every strata, whether it's those in the home, the pulpit, the classroom, the news desk, the judicial bench, and in the halls of government, all have a God-ordained obligation to promote truth and to oppose evil at every opportunity. The past election cycle was especially frustrating in that many pseudo-conservative leaders who could have courageously unified to promote truth chose instead to play it safe, posture, and check which way the winds of opinion were blowing.

The Biden Wish of 2020 Is the Clinton Wish of 2016—Defeat Donald Trump

Hillary Clinton's wish was that Donald Trump would not become president. Joe Biden and his handlers wish that he will not *remain* president. Sadly, many in the Republican Party share that wish. More is said about the improprieties of Trump's private remarks and Tweets than about the security and ethics breaches of Hillary's private computers.

Those in any position of leadership, whether they realize it or not, have an actual charge before God to uphold the greatest common good. This is not always easy to accomplish, and certainly not always popular. But I would have to believe such responsibility would begin by courageously standing with all who would uphold moral law and defend human life.

And pity that so many in church and in government could not sully themselves with a clarion call to flocks and constituents—an inspiring charge to unify around the greatest good.

Prayers will still be answered, and truth will still win in the end. We continue to pursue the good, and as our Founders would advise us to do, looking unto Him who is the foundation of all that is good and true.

5

GUARD THE ROAD THAT LEADS TO DESTRUCTION

Remember the Shel Silverstein book *The Giving Tree?* In that story, a boy selfishly destroys a beautiful tree that he long took for granted. But the tree is so benevolent and kind that even after it has been chopped to bits and is left as nothing more than a stump, it is happy to provide the boy a place to sit. The boy's actions leave the tree (and himself) as near-dead shells of their former selves. The tree personifies character and nobility that the destructive boy learns of only vaguely, and far too late.

In a similar irony, those advocating anarchy, and then socialism as a replacement for our 240-plus-year-old representative republic are working to destroy a force of benevolence and prosperity, the United States of America. Free speech, government by the people and for the people, freedom of conscience, prosperity, opportunity for personal empowerment, and the pursuit of happiness—all of these treasured values hang in the balance right now.

If socialism, militantly secularistic, government-led utopianism continues to spread, the outcome will be that future generations of Americans will not enjoy the things that made America great in the first place. And evidences of liberties lost are increasingly visible already.

Ironically, we are hearing of more lifelong Democrats who are deeply concerned about the future of the Democratic party. The *Wall Street Journal* ran an editorial titled, "Liberalism Isn't What It Used to Be."[14] The piece was written by attorney and law professor Michael Blechman, a former staffer for Robert F. Kennedy and himself a lifelong Democrat. In the article, Blechman looks at how the Democratic party positions adamantly insisted upon today would be largely unknown to the "liberals" of previous generations.

In recent months, words or actions that would trigger apocalyptic levels of outrage had a conservative been guilty of the deeds in question, such words and deeds when portrayed by a socialist/democrat/liberal/progressive are ignored or glossed over. Even when the perpetrator is a fellow liberal (such as when Joe Biden spoke at the funeral of KKK chapter leader Robert Byrd), the outrage is nonexistent. RFK campaign leader Michael Blechman said:

> "Core beliefs that made me a liberal in 1968 put me at odds with many of the things 'progressives' stand for today. Progressives today are running roughshod over much of what liberalism once stood for." He goes on to speak against the selective tolerance of the left, and the militant "identity politics" that favors certain groups with preferential treatment (based on ideological fitness with the Progressive's utopian vision). Conversely, Democrats publicly demonize and treat with contempt other Americans (even to the points of profiling by race and/or

sex)—simply because they might *disagree* with the progressive vision of the left today."[15]

Growing up, most of my family and nearly all of our neighbors were Democrats. But my Democratic relatives and neighbors of previous generations would be horrified to hear California Democrat Maxine Waters calling on party members to publicly harass Trump staff and supporters or make noise at Conservative's homes to interrupt their sleeping. Where is the liberal tolerance in Hillary calling God-fearing, Constitution-honoring Americans "deplorable"? Where is the outrage over Hillary's misogynistic epithet that women who voted for Trump only did so because their husbands told them to? Blechman is right that, "Liberalism somehow made a U-turn when it morphed into contemporary progressivism."[16]

Progressives today act as self-appointed chaperones of American culture. The Democratic party has no place for God or the rule of law, yet it acts as part Holy Spirit, part police force. And for these Dems today, the America that stood strong and proud for 240-plus years must go.

It would be hard to write definitively about any "closely held convictions" of the party today, because other than winning elections by any means, encouraging dependency on the government, and forcibly engineering the direction of culture in accord with Marxist philosophies, there seem to be none. The objective moral truth that Jefferson, the framers of the Constitution, and generations of American leaders knew to be undeniably "self-evident" is completely unknown to Democrat leaders today.

This party of no-morality and fatalism is offering voters ideas that have been proven to fail everywhere they've been implemented. Socialism, globalism, communism, moral relativism—when have these ideological parasites ever improved the nations they've infected? The answer? Never.

Take lessons from observable history. All past nations that have embraced the socialism now being sold to American youth and minorities in 2020 have done a 180, and formerly pro-Socialist nations are in the decades-long process of digging out from the rubble caused by their form of government—the USSR, East Germany, Venezuela, Cuba, China, Poland, Ethiopia, Cambodia, to name a few.

Social Engineering, Socialist Governing

The Democratic party's platform could be part of a tutorial in a class on critical thinking—at least in a lesson on fallacies, which are faulty ways of thinking that lead to incorrect conclusions. The Democrats strongly affirm transgenderism, for example, and have worked relentlessly to erase the traditional binary recognitions of "male" and "female" gender. They literally support legislation that a man can wear a dress and call himself a "woman" and we are all expected to play along, facing potential hate crimes if we do not.

Democrats are quick to label as "bigots" all who disagree with their progressive visions for people and government. But under the platform spelled out on the party website, who would be seen as bigots? Only the world's top leaders, such as Moses, Abraham, Solomon, Aristotle, Jesus Christ, Augustine, Aquinas, Kepler, Dante, da Vinci, Michelangelo, Descartes, Pascal, Berkeley, Galileo, Copernicus, Newton, Lincoln, Pasteur, Shakespeare, Tolstoy, Dostoyevsky, Mother Teresa...not to mention *all* who contributed to the writing and ratification of the Constitution.

The same is true for Fisher Ames, who wrote the First Amendment. All of these people believed in objective moral knowledge, the sacredness of human life, male and female gender, natural marriage, and God the Creator. Were they all fools or villains? The progressive platform—if consistently applied—would lead to that conclusion.

But consistency is not part of the Democrat worldview. Not long ago, many Americans thought that Barney Frank, Al Sharpton, and Jesse Jackson represented the outer fringes of liberalism in America. Now the anger, racism, and illogic daily spewing forth from the voices of AOC, Omar, Tlaib, Nancy Pelosi, and other Dems make "liberals" of old look almost moderate and even patriotic.

Here's the irony. Progressives are using America to destroy America. For pro-Socialist progressives today, the America they hate so much provides them the judicial tools and opportunity to destroy it. The Democratic party of 2020 is using the tools of American democracy to dismantle the very source of their platform and power—our representative republic, once upon a time grounded in morals and truth.

For people of faith, who love both God and country, I believe our Founders would urge us to pray. But for all, more than ever there is the responsibility to be informed and to vote.

Benjamin Franklin said, "A nation of well-informed men who have been taught to know and prize the rights which God has given them cannot be enslaved."

Imagine the earful of social justice platitudes generated if any Democratic party leader today were asked to give their opinion on Franklin's statement. Libraries of progressive critique could be written against his statement, its author, and certainly his peers. It is urgent that God make us a nation of wisdom, moral conviction, and civic involvement.

If Men Were Angels

"If men were angels, no government would be necessary. If angels were to govern men, neither external nor internal controls on government would be necessary. In framing a government which is to be administered by men over men, the great difficulty lies in this: you must first enable the government to control the governed; and in the next place oblige it to control itself. A dependence on the people is, no doubt, the primary control on the government; but experience has taught mankind the necessity of auxiliary precautions."[17] —**James Madison**

Madison understood that "if men were angels" government would be unnecessary. But we all recognize people are not angels. As fallen people in an imperfect world, we require structures and laws to oversee society. Madison also realized, however, the importance of democracy. Government should be both for the people and by the people. This type of check-and-balance system would best help to avoid the extremes of a harsh monarch or moral anarchy.

Yet today, progressives would have us believe anarchy—or at least socialism—is the cool kid in town. Whether the barnstorming speeches of Bernie Sanders or the emergence of new voices like New York's Alexandria Ocasio-Cortez, giving *all* power to the people and treating them as if they were angels appears to be the new Democratic agenda.

Ocasio-Cortez won the Democratic congressional primary in 2018 in her New York district based on the following platform, all listed directly on her campaign website:

- Medicare for all
- Federal jobs guarantee
- Immigration justice/abolish ICE
- Clean campaign finance
- Support LGBTQIA+
- Housing as a human right
- Gun control/assault weapons ban
- Solidarity with Puerto Rico
- Higher education/trade school for all
- Support seniors
- A peace economy
- Criminal justice reform, end private prisons
- Mobilizing against climate change
- Women's rights
- Curb Wall Street gambling: restore Glass Steagall[18]

While some of these issues are noble (such as supporting seniors and women's rights), much of the list sounds like something out of Fantasy Land. Are Americans really ready to let our government guarantee jobs for all, abolish ICE (those who protect our borders), promise a home to every person, ban weapons (in violation of the Second Amendment), and pay for college for everyone? Perhaps the most disturbing aspect of this list is that these views *helped* propel Ocasio-Cortez to a primary victory—one other Democrats and mainstream media gleefully support. Today, many are ready to add to the list the defunding of police, removing the very force designed to protect our communities from harm.

Of course, those who espouse these views often forget one powerful fact—we cannot have true freedom without God.

No Freedom Without God

For roughly a decade, activist-level atheists (such as David Silverman, former president of American Atheists) have organized rallies, purchased billboards, and hit the media circuit trying to relay their message that "One Nation Under God" doesn't apply to all Americans. In one of our first appearances debating together on Fox News, Silverman described the (apparent) plight of atheists in America as one of oppression, discrimination, and even persecution. On air, Silverman lamented that America's ranks of evangelicals would "just as soon see all of the atheists die."

I disagreed strongly, using three reasons as evidence: First, Christians follow the Bible, which teaches us to love people and not wish them to be dead. Second, no Christian would want an atheist to die in a state of unbelief knowing that such persons are spiritually unprepared to face God. Third, I explained that in more than 20 years of interaction with Christians from all denominations and ethnicities, I have never heard a biblical pastor or Christian leader speak with malice about atheists.

Do we wish that atheists would come to faith in God? Of course. Do Christians wish activist atheists would stop their efforts to erase all references to God from American consciousness? Check. Do evangelicals believe that secular activists are effectively undermining other's rights of free speech and of religious expression (You know, the 94% of Americans who believe God exists)? We do. Christians certainly oppose atheism, but none of the thousands of religious people I have ever known have expressed a desire for hurt to come to atheists.

I believe atheistic activism is serving to incrementally kill off the freedoms of others. Therein lies an irony. The Judeo-Christian worldview that birthed America provides a context for atheists to safely live in a state of unbelief. From the writings of our Founders to the brilliant prose of Dr. Martin Luther King Jr.'s 1963 Pulitzer-prize winning work *Why We Can't Wait*, astute thinkers have recognized that God and biblical morality have been part of America's DNA of freedom.

The Judeo-Christian worldview acknowledges that God is the ground of moral reality. Biblical morality (including the precepts of the Ten Commandments) is objective (revealed by God, not arbitrarily "invented" by humans). Because man is made in the image of God, each person possesses inherent worth, value, purpose, and dignity. Each person has God-given rights; and because of their divine origin, our Founders called them inalienable. The underlying belief was that a person couldn't take them away.

Among these rights is the freedom of religious expression. But there is not an inherent right to be shielded from encountering things with which you don't agree. If an atheist doesn't want to believe in God, fair enough, he or she doesn't have to. But a David Silverman or a Michael Newdow should not attack and undermine the very milieu that gives them the freedom to safely live in their state of unbelief. When such activists use political and legal leverage to remove crosses that have been in veteran's cemeteries for decades, or to see all postings of the Mosaic Decalogue eliminated one by one, they are seriously undermining the context of freedom in which Americans have trusted for nearly 250 years.

Activist atheists in America fail to acknowledge that in a free America you must stomach this: We are a pluralistic culture in the sense that you may believe (or not believe) what you wish. But we are (or, at least were) a monolithic culture in the sense that our freedoms are guaranteed protection because they come from God. The agreed-upon presuppositions that made this the land of the free, included beliefs that:

1. God exists.

2. People are made in His image.

3. There are universal rights and wrongs knowable by humans.

When we honor fellow human beings, we are honoring the One whose image they bear. Leaders past and present have reaffirmed these things. In 1781 Thomas Jefferson stated in his *Notes on the State of Virginia*, "God who gave us life gave us liberty. And can the liberties of a nation be thought secure when we have removed their only firm basis, a conviction in the minds of the people that these liberties are of the Gift of God? That they are not to be violated but with His wrath? Indeed, I tremble for my country when I reflect that God is just; that His justice cannot sleep forever."

In 1775, Alexander Hamilton wrote, "The sacred rights of mankind are not to be rummaged for among old parchments or musty records. They are written, as with a sunbeam, in the whole volume of human nature, by the Hand of the Divinity itself, and can never be erased or obscured by mortal power."

In 1924, then President Calvin Coolidge spoke at the unveiling of a statue honoring Methodist leader Francis Asbury. During his speech, he said, "Our government rests upon religion. It is from that source that we derive our reverence for truth and justice, for equality and liberty, and for the rights of mankind. Unless the people believe in these principles they cannot believe in our government."

President John F. Kennedy, in his 1961 inaugural address, said, "The rights of man come not from the generosity of the state, but from the hand of God."

But the telling of American history, according to atheists like Silverman, is that this nation has been a strictly secular, humanistic, godless endeavor. But who is right? Is it the 21st century secularists groping for relevance by seizing media opportunities? Or is it instead people like Fisher Ames, writer of the First Amendment, who desired that the Bible be taught in public schools, because it was an effective vehicle for teaching morality to young people?

Atheists say it is time for their voices to be heard. Fair enough. But just what might that message be? What meaning, purpose, or transcendent mandate do the atheists have to share which we must hear in order to better the condition of our nation? Why do atheists want a seat at the table of cultural leadership, when (in America, at least), the table's guest of honor has been God? Don't care for God? Fine, no one is forcing the atheists to believe anything. But don't erode the very culture that gives you the freedom to disbelieve.

A Matter of Life and Death

Since the Bible is clearly all about life, why do so many Americans, including many Christians, favor abortion—the taking of an innocent life? Let me highlight the main arguments of pro-choice advocates and provide a life-giving Christian response to each one.

Abortion is acceptable because it is legal. There is a difference between what may or may not be legal and what may or may not be moral. The fact that abortion is currently legal in the U.S. does not by definition make it morally right.

Biblical evidence against abortion is lacking or absent entirely. Pro-choice advocates say that if God wanted us to be against abortion, both the Old and New Testaments would contain clear statements against abortion, but they don't. But just because the Bible may be silent or not explicitly clear on a matter does not mean that it approves of the matter in question. Ancient Jews and Christians may not have felt the need to include an open statement against the pagan practice of abortion, because they inherently found it repulsive and assumed there was no need to include a direct statement against it.

What other arguments are used to support the pro-choice view? Ethics scholar Scott Rae offers the following arguments,[19] which I include here with my own commentary on each point:

1. *A woman has the right to do with her own body whatever she chooses.* This takes us back to the overarching debate over abortion—the question of rights. Those who favor abortion see the woman's right as supreme, while those who oppose it champion the rights of the unborn—not by denying the rights of the woman, but by acknowledging that the rights in question have to do with two people, not just one. In other words, choose both!

2. *If abortion becomes illegal, we'll return to the dangerous days of the back-alley butchers.* This is not a valid argument against

abortion, but against the alleged consequences that will supposedly happen if abortion is made illegal. It fails to address the central question—is the fetus a person or not?

3. *Forcing women, especially poor ones, to continue their pregnancies will create overwhelming financial hardship.* Again, this argument doesn't address the key question about whether or not the fetus is a person. This is not a cost analysis—it is a question of life and death!

4. *Society should not force women to bring unwanted children into the world.* Simply because a child is unwanted does not mean that the baby is not a person or does not have any rights.

5. *Society should not force women to bring severely handicapped children into the world.* Percentagewise, very few on-demand abortions that are done fall into this category. This argument also avoids the question of personhood—if the fetus is a person, even one with a deformity or other disability, does that mean such a disabled person doesn't have rights? This line of reasoning puts us dangerously on the path of eugenics—controlled breeding or even the elimination of people deemed not worthy of life. Also, who are we to say that a baby with a deformity or other disability can't live a meaningful, fulfilling life and make positive contributions to society?

6. *Society should not force women who are pregnant from rape or incest to continue their pregnancies.* Do you see a pattern here? This argument also sidesteps the question of whether or not the fetus is a person—an innocent human being with rights of its own. No one is saying that rape and incest are acceptable—they most certainly are not—but as the old saying

goes, two wrongs don't make a right. Why kill a child made in God's image?

Remaining neutral can be tempting for Christians who, out of a desire to avoid tension, don't take a stand on issues like abortion. But abortion involves serious questions about matters of life and death. God has called us to engage culture and use our minds to seek to understand His will in this world. If we remain silent and neutral on crucial questions of our day, we're hardly being the salt or light God has called us to be.

Responding to the LGBTQ Agenda

The person calling my radio program identified himself as a Christian, quickly letting me know he was phoning in to "straighten me out" on what the Bible says about homosexuality. This conversation was taking place on a live broadcast, as breaking news was reporting comments about homosexuality made by *Duck Dynasty*'s Phil Robertson. On air, I had expressed agreement with Robertson's position that Scripture does, in fact, condemn homosexual activity.

According to the caller, it was not that simple. The person asked, "What about drinking alcohol? Christians disagree on that—and on a whole lot of other things. Why can't homosexuality just be one of those things on which believers just agree to disagree?" While I agree there are some areas where Christians can disagree, same-sex activity is not one of them. There are six important aspects of the LGBTQ agenda those holding to natural law would disagree.

1. There's No Room to "Agree to Disagree"

What the Bible teaches about the use of alcohol and what is spelled out about human sexuality are two different things. I pointed out that well-intentioned Christians hold differing convictions regarding the use of alcohol, though all who respect the authority of Scripture would agree that drunkenness is sin. But the caller's analogy failed, because Scripture is unmistakably clear about moral parameters regarding sexuality. And without question, the Bible presents same-sex activity as being sinful.

While I believe that compelling lines of evidence point to the inspiration and authority of Scripture, I know that many people today don't view the Bible as authoritative (just quote the Bible on most college campuses, and you will quickly learn this firsthand). But even apart from scriptural prohibitions against homosexuality, let's consider some of the extra-biblical arguments for and against homosexuality. Let's examine the typical arguments for homosexuality, and we'll weave in arguments from the opposing camp as we go.

2. "Homosexuality Doesn't Harm Anyone"

Those who support the view that homosexuality does not cause any harm are really saying, "Mind your own business!" According to this position, homosexuality harms no one and, therefore, is perfectly acceptable. But if it can be demonstrated that homosexuality does have negative results, then the claim that it doesn't harm anyone is false. Those who oppose LGBTQ practices add that homosexuality does cause harm, especially when it comes to the spiritual condition of the person in question.

3. "Consenting Adults Can Do What They Want"

Proponents of homosexuality often claim that homosexuality is a matter of personal choice between consenting parties. But this claim is just another way of stating the homosexuality-doesn't-harm-anyone argument. It's possible that it does cause harm to individuals and to the culture. It should be added that given moral law, consensual behavior does not automatically mean that the behavior is morally valid. In other words, just because it can be done does not mean it should be done.

4. "Morality Can't Be Legislated"

Supporters of homosexuality typically argue that morality cannot be legislated: "There is no point in trying to legislate morality, so don't bother." But anyone with a sense of what's happening in the world or even occasionally listens to the news knows that in some way someone is always trying to legislate morality. People only consider a given piece of legislation worthwhile, however, if it encourages a version of morality that they support. And if morality can't be legislated, then why do homosexual activists fight to support laws that support same-sex activity?

5. "Homosexuals Can't Escape Genetics"

Many supporters of homosexuality argue that certain people are simply born with homosexual tendencies. No matter what they do, they can't change that fact, so leave them alone and stop trying to "cure" them. But there are serious problems with the theory that homosexuality is genetic rather than learned. For example, if homosexuality is genetic, how have the responsible genes been passed from generation to generation?

Furthermore, if sexual orientation is fixed from birth, why do some homosexuals switch to heterosexuality or bisexuality? Even if it could somehow be proven a person was born with an "orientation" that desired sexual activity with someone of the same-sex, it does not necessarily follow that same-sex activity is positive or beneficial.

6. "Those Who Oppose Same-Sex Relationships Are Intolerant and Narrow-Minded"

Some supporters of homosexuality accuse those who oppose homosexuality as being out of touch, bigoted, and prejudiced. This, though, really isn't an argument in favor of homosexuality. Rather, it's a sentiment that suggests that opponents to homosexuality are unwilling to share their freedom. Unfortunately, this neglects the question of truth. The question isn't about whether a particular emotional reaction to a behavior is correct but whether or not the particular behavior is right, given the available evidence.

How important is it that we defend the biblical position on moral issues such as homosexuality? Extremely so, because the souls of people hang in the balance. If Christians differ on their views about alcohol consumption, environmentalism, or welfare, the result is honest disagreement. But different approaches to homosexuality cross into the territory of heresy.

As our nation wrestles with this issue—and as well-funded, well-organized, tireless propaganda pushers condition the culture to accept homosexuality as a healthy sexual option—we'd do best to approach one another with love, gentleness, and respect as we share what makes the most sense considering God's Word (and good sense).

Blurring Gender Lines:
The Ultimate Form of Moral Relativism

Who would have thought that a retail giant's bathroom policy would ignite a national debate? But that's exactly what has happened, as over 1.5 million concerned citizens have signed an American Family Association #BoycottTarget pledge after the corporation announced that it was restating its bathroom policy. According to Target, transgender team members and guests can use the restroom and fitting rooms of the gender with which they identify.

Gender issues are certainly tied to biblical truth, and the blurring of these gender lines is the ultimate form of moral relativism. The fight against gender is a fight against natural law, and a fight against natural law is a fight against God. What could be more rebellious than to speak against God by declaring to Him, "You have no right over my gender! The Creator doesn't decide my identity, I do!" We are designed by God, and part of that design is, inherently, our gender. It's one thing to disobey God in our behavior, but to deny God in how He created us is another thing altogether.

Triggered, internet meltdown, July 2020: "Woke" defenders of transgenderism were outraged when medical doctors on several continents pointed out online that men are not at risk for cervical cancer, and females are not at risk for prostate cancer. The general reaction from medical professionals: #OnlyFemalesGetCervicalCancer

Only people who have a cervix can get cervical cancer.

> Only females have a cervix.
>
> This is not transphobia. Biology is not transphobic.
>
> 6:54 PM Jul 11, 2020·Twitter for Android

Essentially, the LGBTQ-transgender community is saying God has no claim over them, not even their gender. The blurring of these lines has gone so far that truth has been pushed aside—even the biological truth of the gender with which we were born. Many Americans, as witnessed by the boycott numbers, are being affected by policies they may disagree with—policies put in place for an extremely small percentage of people. We are in the process of throwing away centuries of human history, moral boundaries, and the basis for Western civilization, because for 40 years, coalitions of activists have been dictating how things should be.

In an interview I shared on the progressive radio network NPR on the North Carolina bathroom law, I shared, "This is an issue of natural law. It's wrong to murder, it's wrong to lie, it's wrong to take your neighbor's wife. And also, natural law is the recognition that there are males and females. Now one of the things that's been really pummeled on the American people for the last three decades is a philosophy called egalitarianism, that there are no differences in the sexes. Natural law says look, there are some differences between male and female."[20]

As we'll discover in our next chapter, the road to anarchy is paved with good intentions. Leftist activists may desire to better humanity, but rejecting natural law will not lead to their intended results. Our goal must be to return to America's Constitution, to "hold these truths to be self-evident."

Why the Violence?

Most Americans remember where they were when they heard the news of the mass shooting where 17 people died in Florida after a gunman opened fire at Marjory Stoneman Douglas High School in the city of Parkland. In the aftermath of the tragic news, I shared it's sad that we are making yet another statement about a tragedy in our country that has been played out through violence. News reports tell us that the shooter's fellow students were not surprised by his actions. He was likely a very sad, angry, and disgruntled young man.

His mother had died, he had been expelled from school, and it had likely been pumped into his head that we are evolved and secular, with no moral absolutes. This is the fruit of the secular worldview. If the secularism of the media and the educational institutions of our country are true, what else can we expect? This young man lived out the worldview he was taught; beliefs have consequences. However, if theism is true, we have an answer, and we have a pathway back.

To some, the words may have sounded harsh. While my heart goes out to those involved in this tragedy and other factors are certainly involved, the response remains true. Beliefs have consequences. When a person has been raised to believe his or her life evolved from lower life forms, our human lives are no more important than a rock or a tree. When a person is raised to think there are no moral absolutes and to "do what feels right," a person's angst can lead to actions that cause great harm to others.

Shooting Straight about School Shootings

The rapid growth of school shootings on American campuses has led to a simultaneous response of shock and apathy. On one side, we find ourselves traumatized by teenagers shooting other teenagers, sometimes in our own community. Parents remove their children from public schools, school boards increase security, and churches hold prayer vigils with hopes to avoid another tragedy.

On the other side, we find our culture increasing in apathy toward school shootings. Why? We can no longer keep track of them. From August to May, headlines regularly update us on the latest shots fired, locked-down campus, and statistics of how many have been wounded or killed. If this were not enough, graphic videos and pictures litter the Internet with scenes of blood and bodies, leaving viewers with unforgettable reminders of the violence. Many parents choose to turn off the television and simply talk about something else with their children.

And why does America stand out among all nations regarding school shootings? While school shootings do occur in other countries, they statistically take place more often in the United States. One report notes:

> Two researchers—Jaclyn Schildkraut of the State University of New York in Oswego and H. Jaymi Elsass of Texas State University—analyzed mass shootings in 11 countries, covering the period from 2000-14. Aside from the United States, they looked at Australia, Canada, China, England, Finland, France, Germany, Mexico, Norway and Switzerland.

The United States has more mass shootings—and more people cumulatively killed or injured—than the other 10 nations combined, according to their research. While part of this is because the United States has a much bigger population than all but China, the difference can't be explained by skewed population numbers alone.[21]

The numbers have only increased since the time of this study. America's public schools are increasingly becoming known as killing zones with no clear answers in sight.

An evaluation is certainly warranted. Why are school shootings taking place? Do common traits exist? Anti-gun activists would have us believe the problem is our firearms and the answer is removing guns from American citizens. Yet I remember growing up with classmates who had their hunting rifles and shotguns in the back of their pick-up trucks in the school parking lot in high school. No one was worried about being shot. Guys often carried a pocket knife on campus; students did not feel threatened.

A March 2018 commentary by John Malcolm, vice president of the Institute for Constitutional Government, first provided for me (and many others) an accurate look at the backdrop of today's graphic school violence. He wrote:

> In addition to often exhibiting signs of increasingly violent and dysfunctional behavior, they are significantly more likely than the average population to suffer from undiagnosed or untreated mental illness; they often come from broken homes; and their shootings may be related to economic insecurity.[22]

He notes the three common traits as broken homes, mental illness, and economic security. None of these three factors is directly related to Second Amendment rights.

Instead, Malcolm notes the importance of correcting what can be corrected and improving what should be improved. Improved families would certainly lead to students who feel loved and less likely to act out in violent ways. Mental illness remains a perplexing challenge to our society. Public schools have much room to improve to identify and respond to the many aspects facing today's students. Yet churches also play a role. Children's ministries and youth programs that will work to help every student are not optional—they are essential. Yet few churches even address the many special needs facing parents and their children today, much less the myriad other mental health issues affecting students.

Economic security stands out as an interesting variable. Malcolm's report cites a Northwestern University study citing:

> A major study by criminologists at Northwestern University looked at the effect of economic conditions on the prevalence of school shootings and concluded that there is a significant correlation between periods of increased economic insecurity and periods of increased gun violence at schools.[23]

Whether this involves a student's family situation or his or her own struggles to finish school and find success in life, economic insecurity leads to hopelessness associated with many of the acts of violence in the study.

If we truly desire to help students decrease violence on campus, it begins in the home. The answer is in your house, not the White House.

When husbands love wives and wives love husbands and parents love their kids, trust is developed. This foundation can then work to address issues, as applicable, regarding mental health or economics that often contribute to school violence.

On a side note, these three factors are prevalent in situations beyond school shootings. I've encountered numerous students over the years who have struggled with being bullied by classmates. While I have no study to cite, my experience would affirm the same three factors often apply in the lives of those who bully others.

My friend Keith Deltano speaks as an anti-bullying expert across the country. He has opened my eyes with his message that bullying has become more of a round-the-clock problem since social media has become more of a fixture in young peoples' lives. He says students now go home and get text messages, they go on their social media and they find they're getting flamed. It's Saturday night at 11:30 and a 14-year-old girl is sitting down reading all this nasty stuff. Social media has changed bullying tremendously.[24]

The Uncommon Nature of the Common Core

Another example can be found in the cultural arguments for Common Core education. The alleged goal of this initiative, implemented starting in 2014, was to standardize education and increase the quality of education nationwide. Yet a close look reveals a different agenda. Proponents of Common Core education tend to dismiss naysayers, suggesting their concerns are simply with different ways of doing math or including books some parents don't like. But consider some of the details unearthed in just a brief look.

As a worldview expert, I am immediately drawn to literary content. A glance at recommended books reveal some concerning storylines. For example, one recommended book is *The Bluest Eyes* by Toni Morrison. The introduction includes a rape scene while graphic sexual content is also discussed elsewhere. I'm not sure who believes this is appropriate "literature" for students.

Even the *New York Post* featured an article on one eighth-grade recommended Common Core book called *Make Lemonade* by Virginia Euwer Wolff. One family psychologist referred to its twisted message as "child abuse."[25] The graphic language and sexualized scenes certainly give reason for concern. When did the great classics of American literature get replaced with near-pornography?

Yet the tide seems to be shifting. While 46 states initially accepted Common Core standards, 12 have since worked to repeal these standards. Current Secretary of Education Betsy DeVos has called Common Core "dead." Twenty-four states have "reviewed and revised" their English and math standards. Still, the Associated Press notes, "As of 2018, however, nearly every state that adopted the Common Core during the Obama administration has kept the most important features. Across the country, students will take end-of-year tests that align with the Common Core."[26] Much work remains.

Jesus taught wide is the road that leads to destruction. I believe we are witnessing America's drive down this open road at full speed. We don't need to slow down; we need to stop and turn around! Our current path cannot end well, but we have not reached the end yet. When we know what we believe and live it out, we can bring light into a dark place and bring change still today.

6

KNOW WHAT
YOU BELIEVE

Like all responsible parents, Sharon and Scott Yale were thinking carefully about when to talk with their children about puberty and the facts of life. As committed followers of Christ, the Yales especially desired to impart biblical values to their kids regarding marriage and human sexuality. With their children growing from late childhood to pre-adolescence, the time to talk about such things was fast approaching.[27]

But when their middle-school-aged son came home with a booklet explaining 12 ways to use a condom, they knew public education had beaten them to the punch. "My husband and I couldn't believe how explicit and objectionable the curriculum was," explained Sharon. "And presented without first notifying parents, no less."

The Yales are one of countless couples who have been unpleasantly surprised to discover their kids being taught content that conflicts with their family's morals and values. In the case of their son being exposed to sexual content before they had had an opportunity to inform him first,

Ms. Yale says, "In addition to filling our child's mind with content that we found objectionable, as parents we felt like...a "moment" was stolen from us. My husband and I were going to train our children about these matters on our timetable. A progressive, relativistic sex-ed curriculum (which we later learned was funded in large part by Planned Parenthood) took that away."

But this Christian, civic-minded mom was not afraid to make her voice heard. Sharon and other moms attended the local school board meeting in their Western North Carolina town, voicing their concerns about the explicit curriculum.

Members of the school board, however, did not share their concern. "I just felt like we weren't being heard," says Sharon. "This explicit curriculum was not good for our kids, the majority of parents agreed, and approved curriculums that promoted an alternative message—sexual abstinence—were being ignored."

The Board's response to the request for a curriculum change? "No."

But Sharon Yale is a mom not easily discouraged. She persuaded parents, members of the community, and local media to join her at the next meeting of the school board—along with the pastors of the churches where some board members attended.

It was a defining moment. Continuing to defend an inappropriate sex-ed curriculum before the watchful gaze of their pastors was something the board could no longer do. "They went into session, threw out the curriculum endorsed by Planned Parenthood, and implemented the pro-abstinence curriculum that was best for the kids," Sharon explained. "Some said that we moms played 'hard ball.' But as a Christian, a parent, and a citizen, I had to get involved."

The Call to Personal Involvement

More and more people are calling for the church to reclaim its place at the helm of societal change. My friend Dr. Del Tackett (former leader of *The Truth Project*—a popular DVD-based curriculum that introduced millions to apologetics and worldview training for the first time) often says, "Look in any direction, and in every realm of life, God has spoken."

Tackett asserts that a biblically based perspective may be had regarding the home, the church, the classroom (education), the marketplace (business), the judiciary (law and government), the media (journalism), the arts, and in the sciences. He explains God's revelation touches on the complete spectrum of life—all 360 degrees, in every sphere. Recognizing God's purposes for these realms of life is called a biblical worldview, a Christian perspective on all realms of life.

In past eras, Christians were more eager to follow their biblically-informed convictions, take courageous stands for righteousness, get involved, and ultimately wield significant influence. God's people were the leaders in culture and society, making a difference in many different areas including science, the fine arts, literature, education, politics, and more. This is what was intended by the biblical injunction to be *"salt and light"* (Matthew 5:13-16).

Current Christian thinkers such as David Noebel, Nancy Pearcy, Janet Parshall, James Dobson, and Eric Metaxas, to name but a few, believe that the societal ills of today can be traced to nearly a century of the Western church's failure to teach and defend a biblical worldview. Past cultural leaders such as Francis Schaeffer (philosophy), Charles Colson (politics), Jerry Falwell (education), C.S. Lewis (literature), Mother Teresa (fighter of poverty), Richard John Neuhaus (defender of life), and many others, would certainly concur.

All of these leaders recognized that the church in every age is a mixture of things current and things ancient, the popular and the timeless. The church must give every generation "God's take" on all things social and political. It may not be the assignment we would desire, yet it is the assignment we are given.

Get into Apologetics—Not Apologies

Much of my life is invested in speaking on Christian apologetics. I am not apologizing, but rather presenting and defending the Christian worldview.

The Greek word for apologetics appears several times in the Bible. Usually translated as "answer" and "reason," *apologia* means "a defense." A few of the categories of Christian apologetics include the following:

1. *Textual apologetics*—defending the trustworthiness of the Bible and then presenting the content of what it says;

2. *Evidence-based apologetics*—presenting external data that provide objective confirmation of the Christian faith (such as historical or scientific facts); and

3. *Philosophical apologetics*—exposing the flawed reasoning behind popular arguments against Christianity.

My personal definition of apologetics, fleshed out during these past 20 years of ministry is this:

Apologetics *refers to content and methodologies which may be used by the Holy Spirit to contribute toward the discipleship and mobilization of believers, the evangelization of non-believers so that Jesus Christ is exalted and His Kingdom expanded.*

The following eight verses from the New Testament all include the Greek word *apologia*, a legal term that means "to speak in defense of."

- Acts 22:1 (NIV): *"Brothers and fathers, listen now to my **defense**."*
- Acts 25:16 (NASB): *"I answered them that it's not the Romans' custom to give any man up before the accused confronts the accusers face to face and has an opportunity to give a **defense** concerning the charges."*
- 1 Corinthians 9:3 (NASB): *"My **defense** to those who examine me is this."*
- 2 Corinthians 7:11 (HCSB): *"For consider how much diligence this very thing—this grieving as God wills—has produced in you: what a **desire** to clear yourselves, what indignation, what fear, what deep longing, what zeal, what justice! In every way you showed yourselves to be pure in this matter."*
- Philippians 1:7 (HCSB): *"It is right for me to think this way about all of you, because I have you in my heart, and you are all partners with me in grace, both in my imprisonment and in the **defense** and establishment of the gospel."*
- Philippians 1:16 (HCSB): *"These do so out of love, knowing that I am appointed for the **defense** of the gospel."*
- 2 Timothy 4:16 (NIV): *"At my first **defense**, no one came to my support, but everyone deserted me. May it not be held against them."*

- 1 Peter 3:15 (HCSB): *"But honor the Messiah as Lord in your hearts. Always be ready to give a **defense** to anyone who asks you for a reason for the hope that is in you."*

The goal of the apologist is to glorify God. On this battlefield of ideas, believers are soldiers, fighting to secure hotly contested territories. The souls of people are in the crossfire, and the apologist works to see as many lives as possible brought to salvation in Christ.

If all of this sounds a little lofty or grandiose, be encouraged by the knowledge that one of the most well-known apologetics verses was written by the apostle Peter. First Peter 3:15—quoted by apologists everywhere—was penned not by Paul, the theologian and philosopher, but by plainspoken Peter, the fisherman. Just like Peter, each believer has a role to play. More than ever before, believers must rise to the challenge of Peter's words and equip a generation of believers to "Always be ready."

A verse that does not include the word *apologia*—yet one which definitely deserves notice—is in the book of Jude. Of Jude's 25 brief verses, verse 3 admonishes believers to "contend for the faith" (Jude 3 HCSB). The word translated "contend" in English comes from a word that can mean to struggle for something. The Greek word also is the basis for the word *agonize*.

The implication is that with consistency, effectiveness, and absolute dedication, each Christian is to stand up for this precious message, "the faith that was delivered to the saints once for all." In introducing apologetics to audiences who may be hearing about it for the first time, I often say, "There was only one apostle Paul, and he was an apologist." A careful reading of the book of Acts makes it hard to miss Paul's skill as an apologist-evangelist.

In Thessalonica, Paul *"reasoned* with them from the Scriptures, *explaining* and *showing* that the Messiah had to suffer and rise from the dead," and said, *"This Jesus I am proclaiming to you is the Messiah"* (Acts 17:2-3 HCSB). In his quest to make a presentation of the gospel that was both understandable and persuasive, Paul was explaining and defending his content before the Greek listeners.

The word in Jude verse 3 translated "reasoned" is the word from which stems "dialogue." The word "explaining" means discussing or even disputing. And the word "demonstrating" can also mean to open up something. When a Christian presents, explains, or defends the gospel, the hope is that people will become more favorably inclined to the message, to become *open* to the reality of Jesus Christ.

This same word for "showing" is found in a few other New Testament passages. In Mark 7 we read of Jesus healing a man who was both deaf and mute. In verse 34, Jesus prayed for the man, saying, "Be opened!" This same word in Acts 17:3 speaks of Paul "demonstrating." Jesus gave hearing and speech to a destitute man.

To people who may be spiritually destitute, believers are to give a clear "demonstration" or an "opening." The approach to apologetics should be like that of Paul—something that makes a clear demonstration or opens up others to the truth.

What About Me?

Many believers I know struggle to find their place to get equipped and involved in today's spiritual and cultural issues. Sometimes I share the story of my friend J. Warner Wallace as an encouragement. As a cold-case detective turned Christian, his vocation did not seem to connect with any type of spiritual mission. Yet his life—and work—have transformed into a ministry that is changing lives on a tremendous scale.

Shortly before the spring/summer COVID quarantines of 2020 put our *Truth For A New Generation* apologetics conferences on hiatus, I introduced renowned investigator J. Warner Wallace to an audience in Ohio. Wallace—a cold-case detective who made his own investigation leading to the conclusion that Christianity is demonstrably true—has helped thousands of individuals experience Christianity in a personal way. Bringing him onstage, I told the crowd that, "J. Warner Wallace is one of the most intelligent and methodical defenders of the faith today. As a former atheist himself, this faith investigator understands the skepticism that runs rampant in today's culture...." As he always does, Wallace holds listeners captive with facts and knowledge supporting the never-changing truths of God's Word.

Wallace now serves as an apologetics professor and author of *Cold-Case Christianity* and *Forensic Faith*. Wallace was a conscientious and vocal atheist throughout his undergraduate and graduate work. He considered himself an "evidentialist," and his experience in law enforcement only served to strengthen his conviction that truth is tied directly to evidence. So he embarked on an investigation of Christianity, not only for himself but for others as well.

In Wallace's book, *Forensic Faith: A Homicide Detective Makes the Case for a More Reasonable, Evidential Christian Faith*, he helps readers understand why they have a duty to defend the truth, develop a training strategy to master the evidence for Christianity, learn how to employ the techniques of a detective to discover new insights from God's Word, and become better communicators by learning the skills of professional case makers.

After becoming a Christ follower in 1996, Wallace continued to take an evidential approach to truth as he examined the Christian worldview. Wallace served as a youth pastor for several years and then planted a church in 2006. Along the way, he authored *Cold-Case Christianity* and created the Cold-Case Christianity website, blog, and podcast as a place to post and talk about what he discovered related to the evidence supporting Christianity.

With real-life detective stories, fascinating strategies and biblical insights, Wallace teaches readers cold-case investigative disciplines they can apply to their Christian faith. His commitment to using his abilities to communicate his faith and change culture are having tremendous impact.

Set Realistic, Measurable, and Repeatable Goals

John Wesley (1703-1791), the founder of the Methodist Church, asked the question, "If religion is not extended to the children, what will be the outcome?"[28] Four decades ago, acclaimed historian Will Durant observed that America "was living on a shadow" of its largely-forgotten Christian foundations. Expressing serious concern about the future, Durant asked, "What will happen to our children...? They are living on the shadow of a shadow."[29]

In obedience to Christ's Great Commission, and in a quest to preserve our Constitution and freedoms for future generations, it is imperative that Christians embrace an ethic of citizenship. Translation: "Get involved!" Here are several things to keep in mind:

- Social involvement is not an anomaly, or something for "other Christians" to do; positive cultural impact is what Christ intended for His church.

- Your efforts matter. That letter to the newspaper, the respectful feedback you give a merchant, the phone call to an elected official—these all carry more weight than you may imagine.

- Remember that societal change—good or bad—comes about incrementally. Stay faithful and be patient. The cataclysmic "tipping points" (such as Supreme Court decisions) are virtually always preceded by years of efforts invested by people who believed in their cause.

- Throughout history, the church has been at her best when under pressure. The times in which we live mandate that followers of Christ *unify*. Jesus prayed for this (John 17:21), and the Christian unity that our Savior desires will bring about social change.

- Stay encouraged. The problems of our times appear daunting, and powerful cultural voices are squarely opposed to the gospel. But Christians have the Holy Spirit, prayer, and the truth of God's Word. It's not even a fair fight! God's church *is* on the winning side!

Is It Worth It?

I want to address a concern I continue to hear from many Americans. On my nationwide daily radio show "Exploring the Word" with Bert

Harper, we hear from amazing callers, yet some face deep discouragement. They ask questions such as, "Is it worth it to keep trying? Is our country still worth saving?"

The answer is an unequivocal yes! But with the endless controversies in our nation, including riots in the streets, the toppling of statues, American children literally being taught to hate America, and an unsettling lack of patriotism these days, we begin to wonder if the unequivocal "yes" will be soon be replaced with a wishy-washy "maybe."

Sadly, in many universities and all walks of life, the new generation of young adults is not encouraged to appreciate this nation as previous generations were. Our young people are constantly told how bad America is, and, if not reversed, this continual conditioning to not love America will seriously undermine our national identity and even our national security.

How do anthem-boycotting members of the NFL—who have become millionaires for playing a game—face themselves in the mirror each day? Why do politically leftist Hollywood actors, who make a living by pretending in front of a camera think it acceptable to denigrate the USA that has given them their opulent lifestyle? And why do any of them think that their status gives them the right to preach their subjective beliefs as "truth" to a non-discerning public?

Early Americans gave thanks for the country in which they lived and the abundance of blessings their God provided. Shouldn't we continue this tradition? Regardless of what notch on the political spectrum one might occupy, we must remember that family, friends, neighbors, and coworkers are all much more important than the petty squabbles around the dinner table, water cooler, or on social media. We should not let celebrity opinions dictate our thinking and/or actions.

At the first American Thanksgiving, Edward Winslow gave insight into the day's meaning:

> "Our harvest being gotten in, our Governor sent four men on fowling, so that we might, after a special manner, rejoice together ... Many of the Indians came amongst us, and their greatest King, Massosoit, with some 90 men, who for 3 days we entertained and feasted ... And although it be not always so plentiful as it was at this time with us, yet by the goodness of God, we are far from want."[30]

This spirit of rejoicing was shared in 1621 by a group of pious men and women who had suffered the loss of half their community to sickness and the elements in less than a year. But it can still be said today, "By the goodness of God, we are far from want." Rather than grousing about America at home, church, or social media, we can cultivate a grateful heart and participate in improving our lives, community, nation, and world.

Your Life Makes a Difference

Your service for Christ today will lead to exciting new assignments for the Lord tomorrow. Sharon Yale knows this firsthand. This mom who once made appeals before the local board now sits as a member *on* the school board. She, like us, can move forward confidently in the promise of 1 Corinthians 15:58 that "your labor in the Lord is not in vain."

7

EXPECT
PERSECUTION

After three decades of faithful service to his patients, British physician David Mackereth was not only relieved of his duties, but he was chastised in court and in the press for holding beliefs "incompatible with human dignity." What controversial positions did this doctor hold that rendered his medical experience no longer useful in the 21st century? Mackereth refused to call a male patient (described as being 6'2" tall and sporting a beard) "she" and "Mrs.," insisting that a genetically male patient not be viewed as (or treated as) a female.

Dr. Mackereth is also a Christian. While his scientific bias against gender fluidity was (in mainstream media, at least) controversial enough, the fact that Mackereth also defended his position using Scripture definitely undermined attempts to salvage his job at a Birmingham, U.K., medical facility.

The 21st century is different from all other generations, at least in this way—we are living in the first era of an international attempt to suppress *moral knowledge.* I refer to the widespread cultural abandonment of belief in "natural law." How do we know this is happening in the Western world? In addition to cases like that of Dr. Mackereth, the list of examples grows.

In the classroom, through the media, in our entertainment, and via rigidly enforced corporate policies, accommodation of clear moral truth is being squelched with unrelenting pressure. America's Founders (and thought leaders throughout history) often referred to our knowledge of right and wrong as "natural law." Phrases like "self-evident truth," "higher law," or "the laws of nature and nature's God" were terms used to describe the awareness of right or wrong known to all people.

The Ubiquity and Source of Moral Knowledge

Natural law doesn't mean people always *do* what is right. But deep down, in our conscience, people really do *know* what's right. The human species is uniquely hardwired with the ability to know right from wrong. In his 1943 classic *The Abolition of Man*, C.S. Lewis documented precepts of the moral codes held by major cultures throughout history, all of which strongly echo the Ten Commandments of Exodus 20.

> "No doctor, or researcher, or philosopher, can demonstrate or prove that a person can change sex. My 30 years as a doctor are now considered irrelevant compared to the risk that someone else might be offended." —David Mackereth, MD

"It is deeply disturbing that this is the first time in the history of English law that a judge has ruled that free citizens must engage in compelled speech." —**Andrea Williams,** attorney representing Dr. Mackereth

Humans are moral creatures, yet no scientific theory can account for *why* humans are born knowing right from wrong. The Bible points out that God universally embedded moral awareness within the human psyche. Romans 2:14-15 (NIV) states, "When Gentiles, who do not have the law, do by nature things required by the law, they are a law for themselves, even though they do not have the law. They show that the requirements of the law are written on their hearts."

Human beings of all generations possess innate moral knowledge: "They show that the requirements of the law are written on their hearts, their consciences also bearing witness..." (Romans 2:15 NIV).

Moral awareness makes each person accountable to God, our Creator. In addition to our moral conscience, common sense tells people of all cultures and ethnicities that males and females are different. The increasingly-enforced LGBTQ message is counter-intuitive and counter-reality. Yet pro-LGBTQ activists deem disagreement with their message an act of violence on par with physical assault. Their lobbying of corporations and government entities to make policies more accepting of LGBTQ demands has been incredibly successful.

All this mitigation against morality endangers not only the well-being and eternal souls of people, but it gravely undermines the preservation of the U.S. Constitution. The cultural call to sexual license and gender fluidity is not the innocuous path to personal "freedom" our nation is being led to believe. Abandonment of known truth comes with painfully high costs—the lives and souls of people and our Constitutionally protected freedoms.

Witnessing the Torture of Gender Confusion

One of the jobs I worked during grad school was as assistant manager of a Christian bookstore. Ministry opportunities seemed to walk through the store's door daily, and one unforgettable person we met was named "Russ." He would come to the bookstore many times per week, and he struggled with many things. Physical abuse that went back to childhood had taken a severe toll on this young man.

For Russ, the peace of Christ and a stable spiritual walk seemed very elusive. Russ one day informed us that he was from then on to be called "Courtney." The real answer to his problems, Russ was convinced, was to become a woman. Shortly after, Russ told us that he was now living with people who truly loved him—but only as "Courtney."

He let us know that his new community had a different understanding of Scripture than we had been sharing. His visits to our store became less common. The last time we ever saw Russ, my wife and I begged him to seek counseling.

The newspaper headline reported that Russ's death was an unsolved case. The tragic circumstances surrounding Russs's death will not be repeated here; whether or not he was murdered, committed suicide, or died accidentally was never known.

But in the "gender fluid" climate of the 21st century, this is certain: Christians who tried to help Russ would today be accused of hate crimes for refusing to encourage the dark, destructive identity of "Courtney." For trying to help this young man trust God's design for his life, we would be guilty of "misgendering." We had taken Russ/Courtney into our homes, our lives, and our hearts. But progressives today would say that the Christian context we offered amounted to "acts of violence."

Morality: Unobscured by Cultural Spin

Because there is a universal witness of God written on every heart, Romans 1:20 contains some very sobering words: "People are without excuse." Before the Almighty, we are accountable. Perhaps this accountability to God—and not just ourselves—is why many in our culture wish that there were no "natural moral law." This is certainly what John 3:19 (NIV) indicates: *"...people loved darkness instead of light because their deeds were evil."*

John's Gospel contains the indictment over humankind's love for sin, but verse 16 of chapter 3 records God's intervention to save us from our guilt: "For God so loved the world that he gave his one and only Son, that whoever believes in him shall not perish but have eternal life" (NIV). The most morally correct and wisest choice anyone may ever make is to respond, in faith and obedience.

When Did Christians Stop Talking About Christ?

I've spoken to Christians about the importance of worldview for nearly three decades. However, in recent years I've noticed a disturbing trend. An increasing number of believers are becoming hesitant to share their beliefs.

My inward concern was confirmed in a 2017 Cato Institute study. The Free Speech and Tolerance Survey asked questions of 2,300 U.S. adults, finding 71 percent believe "political correctness has silenced important discussions our society needs to have." And the consequences are personal, with 58 percent stating that the political climate prevents them from sharing their own political beliefs.

It's unfortunate that so many feel they can't speak about their views in our culture. If there was ever a time for the faithful to have a voice in our society, it is now. The fact that our nation has become so hostile toward some beliefs is a sad commentary and a tragic consequence of a culture that touts tolerance, but really only believes in it when views are agreeable to their own.

Similarly, another survey found that with "safe spaces, trigger warnings and microaggressions the norm on many college campuses,"[31] it's not surprising that a recent Gallup/Knight Foundation poll revealed a growing number of college students are concerned about hostility toward free speech on campus—especially students with conservative viewpoints.

More than 60 percent of students said the climate on college campuses "prevents some people from saying things they believe because others might find them offensive."[32] *This news is also disturbing because if our young adults can't express themselves while in college, when they are formulating their beliefs, they won't be able to share their views later in life, even in the face of adversity.*

Standing Against False Charges of Alleged Hate

Another escalating concern in recent years is today's so-called hate speech. Several conservative Christian groups have stood up to defend themselves against false designations and inaccurate inclusion on a "hate group" list from the widely discredited Southern Poverty Law Center (SPLC). Despite its own reliability issues, mainstream media and the liberal left use the SPLC as a resource to undermine Christian and conservative organizations that have nothing to do with hate.

Even American Family Radio, the network where I host the daily, live "Exploring the Word" show with Bert Harper and my weekly apologetics program "Truth for a New Generation," is included on the "hate group" list along with other pro-family, Bible-believing, pro-natural law organizations such as the Family Research Council, D. James Kennedy Ministries, Alliance Defending Freedom, and the Liberty Counsel.

Assigning the moniker of a "hate group" to these longstanding ministries that have equipped and empowered the faithful for decades is not only wrong, it's damaging to society. These organizations have stood up for the biblical definition of marriage and God's design for gender. How that translates into hate of any kind is baffling.

D. James Kennedy Ministries has since filed a lawsuit against the Southern Poverty Law Center for wrongful inclusion on the "hate group" list. The Family Research Council (FRC) defended the legal action in a statement, with Lt. Gen. (Ret.) Jerry Boykin, former U.S. Army Delta Force commander and FRC executive vice president, remarking:

> "The SPLC is an organization that is an attack dog of the Left, they are not a neutral arbiter that is calling balls and strikes. They are on the field playing, pushing an agenda, and anyone who opposes them is slandered and slapped with a hate label. ...This is wrong. It's not the American way. The SPLC is inciting hatred against Christians, which has already led to violence. It needs to stop."[33]

FRC knows firsthand the damaging effects of the SPLC's own hate mongering. On August 15, 2012, Floyd Corkins entered the FRC headquarters in Washington, DC, and shot a building manager with the intent to do much worse. In court documents, Corkins said he chose FRC "as his target after finding it listed as an anti-gay group on the website of the Southern Poverty Law Center" and had planned to "kill as many as possible." In his statement, Boykin added that James Hodgkinson, who gunned down House Majority Whip Steve Scalise in 2017, was a "Facebook fan" of the SPLC.

The Consequences of Abandoning America's Christian Foundations[34]

Our nation is in a spiritual vacuum of our own making, and the sooner leaders recognize the moral chaos and violence this causes, the better. Some of you may remember when the tragic shootings of Columbine were front-page news for months on end. I was newly launched onto the college speaking circuit that spring of 1999. I remember doing media interviews regarding Columbine for many weeks after that tragedy rocked Colorado and the nation. Part of what kept it in the news for an entire year was the fact that such wanton taking of human life—in a public school, no less—was essentially unheard of in America. We weren't yet acclimated to mass murder in places long taken for granted to be safe.

Now, 20 years later, we've seen many senseless bloodbaths in Fort Hood, Denver, Virginia, Newtown, Chattanooga, and Dallas, just to name a few—and the list grows regularly. After a terrorist in Nice, France, used a truck as his weapon of choice, driving into a crowd and killing more than 80, we barely had time to emotionally process the death toll before news hit of the assassination of dedicated law enforcement officers in Baton Rouge. Today's Antifa riots and acts of domestic terror further continue to escalate growing violence in America's streets to shape daily headlines.

We are a nation whose core values begin with a commitment to the protection of the God-given right to life. Remember the Declaration of Independence? It does still exist. But today, special rights are being demanded by some—LGBTQ activists, pro-Sharia Muslims, and Black Lives Matter insurrectionists—while constitutionally guaranteed rights, such as life, freedom of speech, and freedom of religious expression are being denied to others.

America is sadly on the brink of becoming a lawless society. A growing number of voices are speaking of a looming Civil War. Let's pray this is not the case! It is one thing to stand on convictions about the nature of liberty, but it's something else to live as an unhinged libertine. After decades of educating school kids to believe there are no universally binding morals—while at the same time denigrating and undermining the primary institution for imparting moral conviction (the traditional family)—our drift toward anarchy will be tough to correct. Our answer won't be coming from the White House, but from the prayers of God's people in the houses of worship across our nation.

Today, few leaders defend the Judeo-Christian origin of our concept of liberty, though recent White House changes signal some shift in this regard. Many today live from a mindset of "militant autonomy," assuming America was founded to provide total, unrestrained freedom for all. And where the Constitution as originally written doesn't expressly spell out protection for all deeds, demands, or deviancies—the courts may retroactively *project* them in (another reason selection of our U.S. Supreme Court justices is so important). The recent DACA decision that legalized LGBTQ individuals as a protected minority class is a prime example.

If our core value is the absence of core values, why am I surprised when life is no longer considered life? If the only law is that there are no objective laws, how can we rein in lawlessness? Because we've torn down all moral boundaries, it is hard to tell. I would say, "God only knows," but many no longer believe in His knowledge or authority. How can it be, for example, that "Black Lives Matter," but unborn black lives don't matter? Apparently, black lives only matter to some people only after leaving the womb. Do all unborn lives matter? Is human life sacred in all contexts? If so, then no amount of class envy, rage, or stress caused by one's perceived marginalization justifies the murder of my fellow human—born or unborn.

But just as serious as the now-regular terrorist attacks, killings of police, riots, and other incidents of weekly bloodshed in public places have become, we should be equally concerned about the degree to which we have become comfortable with such things. The violence we are hearing reported in the news daily must *not* become the new normal. We must never resign ourselves to the assumption that it is. Never! Gutless, mindless, satanically deluded assassins and acts of violence must not be permitted to control our culture.

Our leaders and the populace must never be "OK" with terrorism. Our children must never grow up thinking that this is "just how the world is." Because we are at least two decades into the political, cultural, and artistic rigor mortis caused by political correctness, it is harder than ever to help young people understand that there was once an America where ethical truth and God were welcome realities. It is challenging to try to convince twenty-somethings and younger that, yes, there was a time when America was safer, the lives of people were more stable and happy, and where economic prosperity was much more widely enjoyed. With only rare exception, this productive season lasted for the better part of two centuries.

I talk with college students and high-schoolers about such things on a regular basis. They stare in near disbelief as I document how, for 200 years-plus, two basic entities guarded and guaranteed the success of this nation and the happiness of its people—the family and the church.

But we don't talk about traditional family anymore, because that is heterosexist, and belief in binary gender is so "backward." The PC-crowd won't even call the main bedroom in a home a master bedroom anymore, as the reference is apparently racist and derogatory. We don't acknowledge that a biblical view of life contributed to our founding and cultural DNA, even though leaders such as U.S. Supreme Court Chief Justice Earl Warren thought so, in 1954 stating that Christianity was "our guiding genius."

Freed from the oppressive chains of the Ten Commandments and traditional values, secularists of the 21st century have finally positioned us to understand the First Amendment's truest intent: To erase from public consciousness the knowledge of God. This is the party line mandated by most of American academia. Secularism promised us liberation, but what we've experienced is godlessness. We are freer, but less—America today is less safe, less stable, and less prosperous.

If America is to be saved from extinction, we must rediscover the source of all life, and who the Founders said made possible our pursuit of happiness: God. Our Founders predicated everything we've enjoyed on the reality of moral truth and on each person's accountability before God. We'd better rediscover these things—and fast. We need a growing number of authority figures who are willing to talk openly and honestly about the bedrock values we were once proud to proclaim. This should begin with leaders in American homes, churches, classrooms, and in Washington. Christianity, if promoted and embraced, will surely preserve this nation from threats within and without. How do I know this? Because for more than 200 years, it did.

Urgently Needed Today: Moral Courage

I truly believe the best response is not to back down but to step up to the challenges of our society. The greatest need among Americans today is not political correctness, but moral courage.

What is courage? Have you seriously thought about this question? Pressed for a definition of courage, most of us would equate courage with some act of bravery in the heat of a dire moment. I remember a church picnic my family attended where a woman dove into the lake to rescue a drowning boy. She pulled the child to the shore, performed mouth to mouth resuscitation, and the young life was saved. Suddenly it dawned on the woman (and others there who knew her), that she was no swimmer and was in fact terrified of water. But seeing a little boy fall in the lake and not resurface, Mrs. Russel forgot herself, dove in, and acted. This was courage.

The Greek philosopher Plato (born around 427 BC) pondered the nature of courage. In "Laches" (one of his *Dialogues*, and pronounced "Lake-ees"), Plato asks some students to define courage. They talk about boxers fighting in a ring—perhaps such an athletic contest depicts courage. But ultimately, Plato defines courage in terms that are very accurate: The wise thinker says courage is knowing the right thing to do and being willing to do it. Plato's take on courage includes, "the ability to know the right thing to do" and a person having the resolve "to do it."

The Bible, a book shown to be God's Word through compelling lines of evidence, has much to say about courage. Scripture frequently teaches that when God is our foundation, we have no need to fear (Psalm 27:1; Psalm 112:7; Proverbs 3:5-6; Isaiah 12:2). Jesus said, *"Don't be afraid; just believe"* (Mark 5:36 NIV). And 1 Corinthians 16:13 says that believers are to *"be courageous."* Ephesians 6:10 teaches that we get this strength from the Lord's might and power.

Numerous Bible figures served God by exhibiting courage borne out of a deep trust in God (a partial list includes Abraham, Joseph, Moses, Joshua, Deborah, Rahab, Ruth, David, Solomon, Esther, Daniel, Peter, Stephen, Paul, John). Church history is the story of believers living lives of immeasurable courage, trust in God, and radical obedience (such as Polycarp, Justin, and Cyprian). From Martin Luther to Martin Luther

King Jr., we are the beneficiaries of the moral courage of centuries of faithful believers. We have the Bible in English today because of William Tyndale (1494-1536), who was burned at the stake for translating the Scriptures. His last words? "Oh God, open the eyes of the King of England!"

There are acts of Christian courage taking place right now of which we will only know when we reach heaven. Certainly, believers in nations under Sharia law must cultivate a courage of which we in America are completely unfamiliar. It is estimated that 100,000 people a year now die for their Christian faith. Apart from a great move of the Holy Spirit in this nation, and unless there is a turning from the contempt for Christianity that seems to be growing in the militantly secular West, the courage of a martyr is something that believers will have to acquire.

Leaving the Comfort Zone

What assignment has God put before you that is "out of the comfort zone"? Are you a Christian who needs the courage to repent of a sinful relationship? Do you need to find help to deal with the impact of pornography in your life? Does the Lord want you to speak with someone about their soul, yet you fear "offending" them? Are you a pastor who lacks the courage to preach about sins like homosexuality or racism?

We desperately need Christians to courageously speak up about issues of God and country—and to underscore their convictions through exemplary living. *Knowing* the right action is rarely a mystery. But as Plato observed, true courage lies in having the willingness to do it.

Speaking Truth That Helps

Some of the most caring people you meet in life are those who tell you not what you may *want* to hear—but what you *need* to hear. Often, a person who gives you a needed wake-up call or word of correction is not trying to be a bully, or is not trying to "get up in your business," but may be someone with a valid point that needs to be heard. The present culture of political correctness and enforced tolerance has often removed from us needed voices of admonition and correction that previous generations would have been wise enough to embrace.

If you dare to disagree on a moral, cultural, or political issue, be prepared to be labeled a "hater" or even lose your job. Free speech is increasingly being truncated through bullying and intimidation on the part of progressives who amount to a type of social justice warrior thought police. There is moral indignation shown by those who abhor the idea of moral responsibility.

But in this land of Constitutionally protected free expression, it is time to remind the misnamed "progressives" that just because someone disagrees with the concept of same-sex marriage, thinks the rise of Islam in the West has been a "net negative," or believes that genetic differences between females and males cannot be changed by mental "identification," does not mean that such persons are guilty of hate speech.

More than 70 years ago, in his seminal work *Nineteen Eighty Four: A Novel,* George Orwell penned a quote that could well have described the politicized delivery of information in the 21st century: "Doublethink means

> the power of holding two contradictory beliefs in one's mind simultaneously, and accepting both of them."

Instead, these convictions are based on logical thought, ethical conviction, and (if they speak up) moral courage. "Enforced pluralism" has brought us to the point that critical thinking skills are becoming latent and moral voices are going silent. Does the proclamation of truth really come with harsh backlash and costly repercussion? Ask Coach Joe Kennedy, a decorated U.S. veteran and high school football coach who was fired for silently, discreetly praying alone after games.[35] Ask Barronelle Stutzman, the florist who has been left financially destitute because she faithfully stood for her religious convictions.[36]

Stutzman's beliefs, incidentally, are right in line with 2,000 years of biblical Christianity. The same Scriptures that motivated Stutzman to respectfully but unflinchingly stand for traditional morality were also held by the likes of Augustine, Aquinas, Pilgrim William Bradford, the framers of our Constitution, the author of the First Amendment, C.S. Lewis, Dr. Martin Luther King Jr., Mother Teresa, and the late Rev. Billy Graham, to name but a few. Were all these leaders "haters" or "phobic"? And yet a 2017 Washington state Supreme Court ruling mandates that as an artist and business person, Stutzman *must* engage in practice with which she disagrees.

America's Founders courageously fought for our rights, and today we must fight to keep them. To stand for truth today, one risks being misunderstood, maligned, and maybe even unemployed. In this land of free speech, studies show that people are now hesitant to talk about their beliefs.

As a U.S. citizen, the First Amendment protects your inherent right to free speech and the government's promise to protect this. Yet more than ever, people are afraid to verbalize many of their convictions about morality, truth, religion, and values. It's a tragedy that so many feel they can't speak about their views in our culture. If there were ever a time for the faithful to have a voice in our culture, it is now. The fact that our nation has become so hostile toward some beliefs is a sad commentary and a tragic consequence of a culture that claims tolerance only when it fits the left's version of reality.

When I think of someone courageous enough to share a hard truth, I think of Mr. Thompson. He was a businessman who attended the Presbyterian church I was part of while growing up. Mr. Thompson volunteered in the youth and college ministry of the church, invested time with us, and I looked up to him.

Off and on during my late teens and early 20s, I participated in church functions, but I was just going through the motions. At church I was a "poser," showing up when there was free pizza and attending just to try to flirt with the girls. At college, I was a partier. Mr. Thompson was gracious, but saw right through me.

While hiking with my buddies at a state park one weekend, I bumped into Mr. Thompson from church. I was embarrassed that one of my youth leaders saw me with a half-downed bottle of whiskey in my hand—plus I was reeking of alcohol. Later, he sought me out and basically said, "Alex, make a choice: Decide if you're going to get your life together, follow Christ, or not."

Mr. Thompson threw down some hard truth that I really needed to hear at that point of my life. The conversation he had with me back then would have probably been grounds for a lawsuit today. But I thank God that during my formative years, Mr. Thompson, and a few others, looked me in the eye and said some things that weren't what I wanted to hear, but what I needed to hear.

The people who spoke moral and spiritual truths into my aberrant young life weren't "haters." They were people of courage, conviction, and care. Our culture still needs older, wiser voices of correction. Recognize your opportunities for courage—and rise to the challenge.

8

EXPOSE THE UNTRUTH OF THE CULTURE WARS

Viewpoint discrimination, subtly (and increasingly not-so-subtly) practiced by Big Tech giants represents a growing threat to our American freedoms. Endless examples could be cited.

From the President's Twitter account temporarily being taken down to the shadow-banning and demonetizing of conservatives on YouTube, we are witnessing an increasing encroachment that is threatening our ability to speak freely about what we believe. Much is being unearthed in the news about censorship from social media groups whose websites and apps mediate a large proportion of today's news headlines.

Twitter, Facebook, and Google are strongly biased against perspectives contrary to progressivism—in other words, moral positions that naturally flow from belief in natural law. Not surprisingly, posts or editorials seen as anti-abortion, anti-gay, trans-phobic, anti-Islam, pro-sexual abstinence, pro-Israel, or pro-America stand at risk of removal, being flagged with a "fact check" violation, rejected from ads, or other forms of social media censorship.

Social Media Titans: Keeping the World Safe from that Radical, Mother Teresa

Even the ubiquitously revered Mother Teresa was blocked by Twitter! In 2017, this quote of hers was scrubbed: "Abortion is profoundly anti-women. Three quarters of its victims are women: Half the babies and all the mothers." The Mother Teresa quote was labeled by Twitter as "offensive."

In 2019, makers of the pro-life movie *Unplanned* (and their 20,000 Twitter followers) were very surprised to discover the film's Twitter account was abruptly taken down. Outcry about this perceived act of censorship led Twitter to restore the account, saying the suspension was "accidental." But on what should have been a strategic moment for viral marketing efforts (the actual day of the film's release), *Unplanned*'s social media platform was crippled. Their Twitter followers numbered less than 200 when their account was finally restored.

It is well known that many postings that don't meet Twitter's "standards" are forcibly deleted. And surprise, surprise: their standards embrace leftist memes while branding as "unacceptable" ideas that are crosswise to the left's core beliefs—pro-gay, transgender, pro-choice, open borders, universal government-run health care, and U.S. submission to the United Nations.

What did Meghan Murphy tweet that got her temporarily suspended? She wrote that "men aren't women," and "women aren't men."[37] In frustration, Murphy posted this response:

> I deleted the tweets in question ... [then tweeted], "Hi
> @Twitter, I'm a journalist. Am I no longer permitted to

report facts on your platform?" I was promptly locked out of my account again, told I had to delete the tweet in question, and suspended for 12 hours. I appealed ... as it seemed clear to me that my tweets were not "hateful," but simply stated the truth, but received no response from Twitter.[38]

Murphy reported that "her account was locked again on November 15" of this year.[39] "She was told she must delete tweets that read: 'Women aren't men'" and other tweets that challenge leftist orthodoxy.[40] Remember, Murphy is not a Bible preaching right-winger. Yet she raised the alarm, saying, "That a multi-billion dollar company is censoring basic facts and silencing people who ask questions about this dogma is insane."[41]

In that same month, Twitter stated that it would ban users who refuse to call transgender people by names or genders that they choose for themselves. This so-called "misgendering," and "deadnaming" (in other words, refusing to acknowledge that a person can change their physiology) is called an act of "violence" by LGBT advocates.[42]

Journalist Meghan Murphy (who is most certainly not a conservative or right-winger) had her Twitter account repeatedly locked and temporarily suspended. She was forced to delete certain tweets that Twitter said "violated [its] rules against hateful conduct," and now she's been permanently banned.[43] Keep in mind that Twitter is a social media platform that, unchecked, has disseminated everything from pornography to death threats.

Twitter has long been in the censorship business, continually monitoring the use of words and phrases the organization believes are politically incorrect. Why do I mention this? Because if you want to believe what is true, if you wish to base your life (and soul) on what is real, you must be more diligent now than ever before. Today, truth is an increasingly rare commodity, and falsehood is a growth industry.

Isaiah 5:20 (NIV) warns of a time that seems very much like the current day: *"Woe to those who call evil good and good evil, who put darkness for light and light for darkness, who put bitter for sweet and sweet for bitter."* Cambridge anthropologist Joseph Unwin (1895-1936) is frequently cited by those concerned that the West's loss of morality points to a future of anarchy and lawlessness. Unwin is most famous for his 1934 work, *Sex and Culture,* that concluded the stability of a nation is directly tied to the degree of moral and sexual restraint present.

Observation of diverse civilizations throughout 5,000 years of history led Unwin to posit that a common cycle manifests itself in societies: Moral restraint leads to prosperity, but prosperity leads to decadence. Decadence and sexual license ultimately unravel the structure, stability, and prosperity that years of discipline had accomplished. Unwin believed that when moral decadence became dominant in a people, an irrevocable tipping point had been passed. The culture would die.

Interestingly, Christian leader John Wesley (1703-1791) had predicted basically the same thing nearly 150 years prior to Unwin. This founder of Methodism (whose 18th century revival in England created social restoration that would benefit Europe into the 20th century) observed the following:

> "Christianity, true Scriptural Christianity, has a tendency in the process of time to destroy itself. For where ever true Christianity spreads, it must cause diligence and frugality, which, in the natural course of things, must beget riches! And riches naturally beget pride, love of the

world, and ever temper that is destructive of Christianity. Where ever it generally prevails, it (ultimately) saps its own foundation."[44]

Like Nineveh in the Old Testament, America finds itself in a state of self-inflicted guilt and turmoil. The more I think about it, I believe that America is *a lot* like Nineveh: pagan, immoral, ripe for judgment, but with potential for revival. Nahum 1:9-11 warns of the impending judgment that would befall Nineveh, and to a degree the punishment was that God allowed the people to experience the results of their own immorality. Prior to the arrival of Jonah, their God-sent evangelist, the Ninevites were described as being headed for destruction (v. 9), tangled up like thorns, drunk and empty, and like dried up straw, ready to burn up at the slightest spark (v. 10). Nineveh was home to a "wicked counselor" who not only led the people away from morals and truth, but wanted to plot against God Himself (v. 11).

Perhaps America will quickly decimate, as Joseph Unwin's model predicts. Perhaps our nation will experience a recovery of moral awareness and a thirst for truth. It will take the Holy Spirit of God to initiate this. Are you willing to play a role? Let me share three things we must always keep in mind during times of chronic falsehood.

First, all people are called to accept what is true. Conversely, we are called to flee what is false. Therefore, we need wisdom! Proverbs 8 describes wisdom as a woman crying out in public. It is as though truth is begging us to follow wisdom!

Second, we are to commit to what is true and invest our lives in truth. The psalmist wrote, *"O Lord, who shall sojourn in your tent? Who shall* *dwell on your holy hill? He who walks blamelessly and does what is right and speaks truth in his heart"* (Psalm 15:1-2 ESV). That takes commitment.

Third, we are to proclaim what is true. The prophet Zechariah cautioned, *"These are the things that you should do: speak the truth to one another..."* (Zechariah 8:16 NASB). In these ever-changing, increasingly censored times, are we accepting the truth? Are we committed to it and proclaiming it? Do we correctly understand what God asks of us?

God wants us to believe in Him and love one another. When we do these things, other people take notice, whether they accept our beliefs or reject them. Matthew 5:16 (ESV) teaches, *"In the same way, let your light shine before others, that they may see your good works and give glory to your Father who is in heaven."*

Our goal is not to point people to *ourselves* but to Him, bringing glory to our heavenly Father, who is truth.

Remember When People Respected the National Anthem?

The 2017 NFL season was not marked by the usual dazzling highlights, but rather what happened before the kickoff. The controversy even rose to the highest levels of our nation, with President Trump speaking out against the pre-game practice of kneeling during the National Anthem.

Vice President Mike Pence took a stand of his own one Sunday afternoon by walking out of the Indianapolis Colts-San Francisco 49ers game when several players kneeled during "The Star-Spangled Banner." In his statement, "I left today's Colts game because President Trump and I will not dignify any event that disrespects our soldiers, our Flag or our

National Anthem. ...At a time when so many Americans are inspiring our nation with their courage, resolve, and resilience, now, more than ever, we should rally around our Flag and everything that unites us. While everyone is entitled to their own opinions, I don't think it's too much to ask NFL players to respect the Flag and our National Anthem. I stand with President Trump, I stand with our soldiers, and I will always stand for our Flag and our National Anthem."[45]

Another discouraging factor weighing during the kneeling protest controversy was when young football fans looked up to their favorite players, emulated them, and copied their actions. During the 2017 football season, a survey showed how Millennials viewed the protests, with a slight majority supporting the athletes' actions. *The Washington Post* cited the GenForward Survey, which found that 54 percent of young people say that kneeling during the national anthem is acceptable. When race is taken into account, the numbers vary greatly.[46]

In general, young people are finding their way and discovering who they are. They can be heavily influenced by media, culture, and their peers. But they also take to heart beliefs by their parents, teachers, professors, pastors, and church leaders, who can speak truth into the most controversial societal issues of today. These are teachable moments, when we can talk to Generation Z about respect, commitment to country, a knowledge of history, and what our actions say to those who built this nation and fought and died for our freedoms. Yes, they also fought for the freedoms of peaceful protest—all the more reason we should stand for the flag and National Anthem, regardless of our age, background, or place in society.

I don't doubt that most if not all NFL players realize that their youngest fans are watching them every minute of every game, both before the clock starts and while they make plays. Maybe some want their young fans to see them disrespect the flag and the country—for whatever reason, to prove a point or teach a lesson they think should be learned. But those who stand and show respect, no matter how they might feel about the state of the nation, also teach a valuable lesson.

Ultimately, it's up to parents and perhaps coaches to explain to young athletes why their sports idols are sitting, standing, kneeling, or raising fists. We must never let a teachable moment slip by; but instead, we should turn these Sunday afternoons into times when we can talk to kids about patriotism, respect, and the responsibility of those who are in the spotlight. I hope these players know the negative message they are sending to America's next generation with their actions.

As an example, a group of 8-year-old football players decided to kneel before their game in late September after learning about the unrest and violence in St. Louis. The coach of the team in Cahokia, Illinois, said his players began asking questions about the riots, reported on SBNation.com.[47] Though these young players may not fully understand why they were even kneeling, their actions signal a new frontier in our society, one in which even our youngest athletes are pressured to show disrespect toward the very people who have fought and died to secure the freedom of our nation.

What Drives a Culture?

In 1975, Christian leaders Bill Bright and Loren Cunningham met for the very first time. It just so happened that God spoke to each of these leaders that very week about the importance of the seven cultural spheres, or mind molders, as Bill Bright called them, necessary to impact the culture for Jesus Christ. These seven areas were business, government, media, entertainment, family, education and religion.[48] In this chapter, we'll take a brief look at the influence of these seven areas.

Instead of "mountains," however, I speak of these seven areas as "engines." Why? In a car, the engine determines the power and direction of the vehicle. The better the engine is designed and maintained, the more effective the car will travel. When speaking of seven engines that drive culture, we'll discover some of the ways these engines have been manipulated for negative purpose, as well as examples of how to use them for godly impact.

Engine 1: Business

Religious freedom is a bigger issue in America today than some realize, touching every area of society, including business. In recent years, the notion of religious liberty has become increasingly contentious because of a growing cultural divide over faith and its place in the public square.

In 2017, the Supreme Court decided to take up the case of a Christian baker who did not make a cake for a gay couple's wedding.[49] Jack Phillips, owner of Masterpiece Cakeshop in suburban Denver, Colorado, claimed religious exemption due to his belief in traditional marriage.

The ability of our citizens to actively and freely live out their religious beliefs is a vital part of the American dream. A majority of evangelical Christians say religious freedom is what makes America great, according to a study released from the Barna Group, an evangelical Christian polling firm based in Ventura, California: "Though the idea of American exceptionalism isn't a recent invention, we've heard a lot lately from

President [Donald] Trump and his supporters about 'making America great again.' But what, exactly, do people believe makes America great?" the organization asked in its poll of 1,015 adults, taken from June 5 to 9, 2017.

Fifty-three percent of evangelicals said they viewed religious freedom as the key quality that makes this country great, the group reported. On average, 20 percent of Americans hold this view.[50]

"Evangelicals esteem freedom of religion and America's Christian roots more than any other group," Barna noted. Forty percent of evangelicals viewed America's Christian roots as making America great again—compared to an 11 percent average from respondents in the poll.[51]

In the case of the Christian cake baker, the court decided the fate of his American dream. Fox News framed the case with the words prior to the decision: "The high court will now decide whether applying Colorado's public accommodations law to compel the baker to create 'expression'—a wedding cake—violates his constitutionally protected Christian beliefs about marriage.... Phillips told the Supreme Court he has free speech and religious rights under the First Amendment that should protect him. He said he should not be compelled to bake a cake specifically to honor a same-sex marriage."[52] In 2018, Jack Phillips would win his case, marking a new religious liberty victory for conservative small business owners.

Engine 2: Government

Much more could be set forth in documenting the influence that biblical values and Christianity played in the nation during times past. Documentation could be given regarding what America's Founders saw as the necessary role of religion in public life. But regarding the issues of our day it is important that we ask, "What might the Bible have to say to me about citizenship here and now?"

The Bible is clear that the "powers that be" (governments) are permitted/sanctioned/allowed by God. Despite news reports that appear to the contrary, God is very much in control! Christians are not to be insurrectionists or part of some resistance movement. We are to submit to governmental authority: *"Let every person be subject to the governing authorities. For there is no authority except from God, and those that exist have been instituted by God"* (Romans 13:1 ESV).

Since our government permits registration of voters and the right to cast a ballot, I believe that Christians have an obligation to vote. Ignoring the privilege (and duty) to vote is, I believe, to be less than faithful in the handling of our Christian responsibilities. The precedent of choosing godly, representative leaders goes all the way back to the Old Testament. God told Israel to, *"Choose for your tribes wise, understanding, and experienced men, and I will appoint them as your heads"* (Deuteronomy 1:13 ESV).

It is estimated that more than 170 million Americans profess to be Christians. However, it is likely that only about one half of these professed believers were registered to vote (or voted) during the 2016 elections. As I travel and speak, I hear various explanations about why Christians do not have a responsibility to vote, or ought not to be involved in politics at all. Many a sincere person has gently reprimanded me, a minister, for speaking about political issues!

Yet we must care enough to get involved in government. In 1984, then President Ronald Reagan said, "Politics and morality are inseparable... religion and politics are necessarily related...our government needs the church." I am convinced that our nation urgently needs a spiritual, moral, and social turnaround. Think of it—your life can be used by God to contribute toward this goal. The prayers and influence of God's people have in times past made a great difference. This will be the case again if God's people rise to the challenge and become involved.

My prayer is that every eligible American will be informed on the issues, will make the effort to be registered, and will do what people in many other countries long to do—vote. It is vital that citizens be citizens, and exercise this God-given right!

Engine 3: Media

Do you remember when the nightly news actually reported the news? Today, however, news outlets seemingly compete for who can "invent" the best breaking scoop—regardless of whether the information is accurate. Worse, each channel or network typically reveals such blatant bias that we might as well label each network Republican or Democrat.

The media's "creative license" with today's societal agenda also extends far beyond news channels. A friend recently commented to me, "Do you remember when MTV used to play music and ESPN used to show sports?" Partly joking, his question highlights the growing trend of politicizing every outlet and activity—often with a biased mainstream agenda attached.

Recent years have addressed this trend to some degree by popularizing the term "fake news." Though truly fake news is a problem, the greater concern tends to be among those who mix fact and fiction in broadcasting today's events. For example, the American public has yet to learn what really happened at Benghazi. The short "news" account labeled it as an attack on American troops in retaliation for a YouTube video from a small-scale video maker in California.

Conservative Christian journalists are sorely needed throughout the spectrum of today's media, though are increasingly overlooked by mainstream media. Instead, new forms of media are arising, from the Blaze to CRTV's streaming subscription model, next-generation conservative outlet DailyWire.com, and independent journalists reporting direct to social media channels. The Internet remains a "Wild West" of reporting activity, leading to the best (and worst) of media in our nation's history.

Engine 4: Entertainment

Entertainment saturates our culture. Many of us spend far more time with our screens than with our spouses—or anyone else for that matter! We need no convincing of the influence of media. However, we may need a reminder of its power, both positively and negatively.

Have you ever been to Magic Mountain, the famous amusement park in Southern California? It was long known for a roller coaster named X. Coincidentally, I was there to speak at a youth event when I overheard an X-rated conversation between some teens who were part of a church youth group. Later that day, the conversation prompted me to address the issue from the stage. I asked, "How many of you struggle with using bad language?" Many hands went up. I followed up with questions we've all probably considered at some point: Is it wrong for a Christian to use curse words? If so, why? And what makes profanity, well, profane?

Entertainment is full of swear words, sexual innuendo, and scatological slang. In one study of primetime TV, the Parents Television Council identified more than 11,000 expletives—twice as many as were used a decade ago. Indeed, in our coarsening culture, some young people can't recall a time when f-bombs weren't part of "normal" discourse. Kids use it because they've grown up hearing profanity and having it reinforced by the media. And somehow it becomes a personal habit that even Christian teens may consider acceptable.

I've heard people argue that words are just sounds to which we attach meaning. But to deny the power of language, one must argue the point with what? With words. And those combinations of letters and sounds assume that meaning will be conveyed, heard, and grasped. You assume that your listener understands what you're saying. We can't get around the fact that words contain meaning.

The Bible reminds us that our words should honor God and benefit others. Ephesians 4:29 (NIV) says, *"Do not let any unwholesome talk come out of your mouths, but only what is helpful for building others up according to their needs, that it may benefit those who listen."* James 1:26 warns us to keep a tight rein on our tongues, while Colossians 3:8 says, *"rid yourselves of all things such as these: anger, rage, malice, slander and filthy language from your lips."*

Regarding the use of profanity by believers, some contend that since Christ makes us free, how we say things doesn't matter. While salvation sets us free from the penalty of sin, *freedom* doesn't equal *license*. In fact, the Bible makes it clear that Christians have an obligation to pursue holiness (Ephesians 4:24; Titus 2; 1 Peter 1:5; 2:24). Indeed, God's ownership of believers extends even to the words we use. According to 1 Corinthians 6:19-20 we're mere stewards. Jesus Christ owns us, including our minds and mouths. Spiritual maturity requires that we yield everything to God.

All Christians should submit their vocabularies to the lordship of Christ, in part because God is always listening. His grace is perfect, but if words didn't matter, Jesus wouldn't have said, *"I tell you that everyone will have to give account on the day of judgment for every empty word they have spoken. For by your words you will be acquitted, and by your words you will be condemned"* (Matthew 12:36-37 NIV).

Profane means "unholy" or "unwholesome." Some types of speech are literally unholy. Spouting certain four-letter words can hinder spiritual growth, harm relationships with others, and undermine our credibility as bearers of gospel truth. Christians possess an advantage by having a pure well of words from which to draw.

Years ago, as a new believer working my way through college, a superior took note of the fact that I didn't tell off-color jokes or use foul language like others in that workplace. Not only did this create a witnessing opportunity, but I was promoted to a level that no 21-year-old had ever held in that company. My boss later told me that my habit of avoiding profanity led him to promote me. Words have power, and today's media often serves as one of our major learning tools for our daily vocabulary. We would do well to use our words—and our entertainment—wisely.[53]

Engine 5: Family

A disturbing poll's results suggest that America is becoming even more racially divided.

According to a CBS/*New York Times* poll in 2015, Americans believed race relations were at their worst point in more than 20 years, with 61 percent saying race relations are "bad"—the highest percent since 1992.[54] The poll also marked the first time since 1997 that majorities of both white and black respondents believe race relations are poor.

As the country focuses on race relations today, few are courageous enough to address one root issue: family instability. Young people in America—and particularly young men—who grow up in unstable homes are angry and frustrated. They don't understand why things are the way they are. Indirectly, racial tension is often an expression of frustration and anger over the absence of family stability. Does racism exist? Tragically, yes, and we would be blind and naïve to say it has been fully eradicated. However, when we see expressions of violence stemming from racial tension, we often see behind it the breakdown of the family.

Current societal attempts to address racial tension fail to get to the root of the issue, and government efforts, particularly, have often exacerbated rather than helped solve the problem.

For more than four decades, political leaders have preached a gospel of race and class envy while encouraging family breakdown.

As economist Thomas Sowell so boldly notes, liberal policies supposedly meant to raise people up have in truth promoted the destruction of families, and particularly of African-American families. Whereas in 1960, the majority of African-American children were being raised in two-parent households, just a few decades later, most have been deprived of at least one parent. Couple this with a prevailing political philosophy that one person's success necessarily means another's failure, and it's little wonder that frustration and anger result.

Is America facing a crisis of racial division? Yes. But it is being perpetrated rather than resolved by policies that continue to promote race and class envy while failing to focus on the root issues: morality, accountability, and most importantly, the restoration of the family.

Engine 6: Education

In a publication regarding the Bible in public schools, I shared that bringing biblical education back to our classrooms is exactly what our country needs.[55] The Bible, whether people want to believe it or not, is the book upon which our country was founded. These valuable Bible classes in our high schools don't have to teach Christianity to be successful. To give students a working knowledge of the Bible, whether for spiritual or academic reasons, will help restore our country to those founding biblical principles.

I've heard some people lament regarding the inflated cost and decreasing return on investment from public colleges as well, saying, "College costs four years and $100,000 to discover that you can't know anything."[56]

Over a decade ago, in his excellent work *Brainwashed*, author Ben Shapiro observed that a college "education" at many universities today amounts to "a four-year attack on America and God." Shapiro's raising of a different perspective—no matter how scholarly in presentation— meant he had to be silenced. Shapiro had been fired from the UCLA *Daily Bruin* for writing an op-ed piece around the radical idea that the nation of Israel should not be forced by the UN to give up land for peace. Though extortion-like "land-for-peace" agreements have never brought lasting peace to the Middle East, and though such arrangements have never served the best interests of the nation of Israel, approval of such has been the accepted party line for much of Western academia for years. Shapiro's raising of a different perspective meant he had to be silenced. And he was. More than a decade after the fact, Shapiro's book remains a captivating read.

When the riots at the University of California, Berkeley, over a conservative lecturer coming to campus were reported in the news concerning Ben Shapiro, I was concerned for my country, but certainly not surprised. Over two decades of following campus trends, research, writing, and my own speaking experiences at universities have amounted to a stark education in what more parents need to know—unless you send your child to a solidly Christian and/or conservative college, there's a very good chance you'll be spending your hard-earned savings for a four-year, politically correct indoctrination program.

Liberal arts education has become anything but liberal, as "liberal" in this case was originally intended. At PC-driven schools like Berkeley, the term "university" should more honestly be rendered "monoversity." History is revised, Western civilization is denigrated, while Christianity is ignored or mocked, Darwinism goes unquestioned, voicing your conservatism will get you "failed," and it is a "given" that traditional values are to be abandoned. Free thinking is not so free after all.

College education is less about the pursuit of truth and more about imparting a carefully guarded, often forcefully imposed narrative of economic socialism, political globalism, moral relativism, militant secularism, and personal meaning through hedonism. Unless your children are reading prodigies who have steeped themselves in the great traditions of Western thought, and unless your students have rigorously mastered critical thinking skills, are able to spot contradictions, fallacies, and outright lies for themselves, the undergrad degree will effectively be a programming exercise designed to turn graduates into compliant "worker bees" for leftists.

And parents, don't think for a minute that your child's college education will be different because you are sending your son or daughter to a school that has been historically religious or is tied to a particular denomination. Having spoken at numerous campuses across the nation, I know firsthand that some of the most vehemently liberal schools were built one or more centuries ago by some branch of Christianity. When historically Christian colleges trade "liberal arts" for "liberal agenda" it is tragic, as is the effect they have on young lives.

I remember being scheduled to speak at a historically Methodist school, and being canceled on the day of the event. The president pleaded with me to "understand," saying, "You'd thank me for canceling...I have an insurrection on my hands."

Oddly, this particular school had hosted a Wiccan wedding in its chapel only weeks before my scheduled lecture. I wonder what John and Charles Wesley would think of a school where faculty, students, and administration were okay with an occultist ceremony presided over by a witch, but would refuse to hear what a Christian educator, author, and minister might say.

Imagine a Baptist university where we had scheduled a speaker to give a lecture on the fossil record. This university, known for making much of its Baptist heritage, had in its speaker series a lecture on gay poetry by a presenter who only had an undergraduate degree. At the request of some students, and working through approved university protocols, our ministry helped bring a geologist to campus who was to lecture on objections to Darwinism from within the scientific community.

Then a major pushback and petition was signed by many professors. They demanded this speaker be canceled on the grounds that a person who questioned evolution was clearly "not scientific." In the local newspaper, representatives from the faculty accused this speaker of not being "an academic." We pointed out that his PhD was from Oxford. Again, it's the irony of 21st century higher education—at a historically religious school, a gay poet with a bachelor's degree is welcomed, but a PhD whose research might possibly undermine Darwin must *not* be heard.

G.K. Chesterton, a renowned Christian scholar from a century ago, wrote of "the white horse of truth," which though scarred and wounded would ultimately stand tall and unvanquished at the end of time. This is an encouraging thought when colleges hold so many issues sacrosanct and *absolutely* off-limits for critical discussion or question: global warming; sexual orientation; abortion; the nature of morality; capitalism vs. socialism; American exceptionalism; diversity; Islam; and terrorism. For too many unsuspecting students, and their beleaguered benefactors who pay the tuition bill, the pressure is to question nothing and to comply completely.

Engine 7: Religion

"Christianity cannot be true because of the evil and suffering in our world." That sentiment seems to be echoed today on the controversial front page of the *New York Daily News*, on December 3, 2015, which declared regarding the deadly terrorist-inspired shootings in San Bernardino: "God Isn't Fixing This."

Well, what do we expect? God is just and His justice prevails, along with His love and mercy. But God is not weak or soft, and in a nation that has turned its back on Him, suffering will occur as a consequence.

First, prayer to Almighty God is a serious act. Just because we don't live in a peaceful world doesn't mean that God isn't hearing and answering our prayers, and it doesn't mean that He is not at work. But the truth is that we live in a fallen world, and many want to reap God's blessings without dealing with His judgment. One myth about Christianity is that if God was real, He wouldn't allow bad things—like mass shootings, sickness, and death—to happen. But the truth that counters the myth is that Christianity offers the best hope and power to deal with suffering.

Second, we also need God's protection. This bloodshed on American soil will continue until we genuinely turn back to God. Our leaders must promote morality, natural law, and the Ten Commandments. There is the easy way, to follow God's precepts in our leadership, or the hard way, which is to continue to fight truth and refuse to acknowledge the reality that our world is lost without God. Will we humble our hearts or harden our hearts? The American people and its leadership have accountability in the events that take place on our homeland.

These seven engines that drive our culture stand not as a mere intellectual discussion. The fabric of our nation's values is at stake due to the influence of these areas. If we truly desire for America to be the land of the free and the home of the brave, we must invest our time and resources into developing strategies to improve society in education, business, government, and other key areas of life.

9

STUDY THE PAST TO REDEEM YOUR FUTURE

Our culture tends to be pointing toward the false dichotomy of "Either God or Patriotism." But when did we have to choose one or the other?

When Christians get involved in politics, great things can happen. In many ways, progress on behalf of America and the spread of moral truth depend on it. Some of history's most fortuitous turns resulting in the betterment of the human condition have come about when followers of Christ inserted themselves into governmental and cultural affairs.

Many today, however, would vehemently disagree with that statement. During a recent gathering of leaders from the Southern Baptist Convention, America's largest Protestant denomination, attendees hearing Vice President Mike Pence share his Christian testimony artfully tweeted their disapproval. They took to social media, exclaiming that their allegiance was to God, not man, and their priority was the gospel, not government. For many zealous Christians today, the church's position in relation to politics amounts to one of two choices: *Either* you love the Lord and His kingdom, *or* you have "gotten in bed with the state," and supposedly have your eyes only on this world.

Dichotomizing the landscape to only these two options is unnecessary, inaccurate, and even dangerous. Perhaps, as Augustine taught, believers really are accountable to both the "city of God" and to the "city of man."

For a Christian believer, of course they agree their true home is heaven. Certainly, our number one priority is to proclaim the good news of Jesus, and consistently show forth the love of God. That's why Christians call it the Great Commission (Matthew 28:18-20). But should the church be politically vocal, and can we do this without compromising our loyalty to our King Jesus and His kingdom? Absolutely! We have inherited many blessings today from courageous Christians before us who were intensely politically engaged.

Consider Melito, an ancient Christian leader and pastor from Sardis (now Turkey). In AD 175, Melito met with Emperor Marcus Aurelius, urging him to make Christianity the official religion of Rome. Melito reasoned that, "Church and state were complementary works of God for mankind's benefit."[57] He saw no conflict in meshing Christian beliefs with political discourse.

Many have heard of William Wilberforce and his crusades before Parliament to end slavery in Britain. Perhaps less well-known is his colleague, Thomas Clarkson. Together, they acted on their deeply held Christian convictions, speaking publicly about (and to) the British Empire. They successfully engaged the help of Parliament member Thomas Buxton in their establishment of abolitionist societies, their work on behalf of child rights, and ultimately, the ending of slavery. I think we would agree it was beneficial for these leaders to engage in political and cultural involvement!

In his book *Discovering an Evangelical Heritage*, historian and theologian Donald Dayton documents the pronounced political involvement on the part of Christian converts during the Second Great Awakening during the 19th century. Dayton notes that evangelists such as Charles Finney were, "...instrumental in adding thousands to the active ranks of American churches," but also urged that, "...these new converts become active participants in every forward movement of their time."[58]

The bottom line—do we serve God and merely wait for heaven, or do we immerse ourselves in current events and cultural involvement?

The answer is both! For those who advocate political disengagement, it is helpful to remember all the immeasurable good accomplished by Christians courageous enough (and wise enough) to understand the church's responsibility to a lost world. I think again of the servant of the poor, Mother Teresa; civil rights reformer, Dr. Martin Luther King Jr.; evangelist Billy Graham; educator Jerry Falwell; prison ministry champion Charles Colson. These are only a few of countless men and women who have lived out their faith in society to make an impact now and for eternity. May the Lord empower us to also make a tangible mark for Christ in our world today—but also in our government as well.

Moving Beyond Safe

Of the millions of American Christians who attended church last weekend, how many are still reflecting on a hard-hitting Sunday sermon their pastors delivered just a couple of days ago?

Probably not many. The reason? More and more pastors are resorting to covering the "safe" topics in today's American churches.

It's time to call out many pastors for what they've become: B-grade motivational speakers. The excuses are many: people will be offended; giving will decrease; leaders will leave the church; and many more. But there should be no excuse for not preaching on the most critical issues of our time in today's American church. We can't hear truth in the mainstream media or anywhere else in society. Society is counting on the church to explain God's take on moral issues, political issues, and hard truth in an honest, relatable way, even if it is uncomfortable. As ministers, we must not fail in our duty to proclaim truth!

Research backs up these observations. In 2017, the American Culture & Faith Institute polled 600 Protestant pastors about how often they had preached about the top culturally relevant issues. The results were dismaying. In fact, between the 2014 and 2016 elections, the percentages of pastors who addressed these hard-hitting topics plummeted.

For example, in 2014, 48 percent of pastors preached on the topic of abortion, but two years later, just 26 percent tackled this issue. Numbers were similar for other issues as well: immigration (17 percent in 2014 vs. 8 percent in 2016); Israel (24 percent in 2014 vs. 11 percent in 2016); religious freedom (63 percent in 2014 vs. 36 percent in 2016); and Islam (38 percent in 2014 vs. 13 percent in 2016).[59]

We are witnessing the unraveling of Western civilization. Now is the time for pastors to deliver the most powerful sermons of their lives and to argue on the matters important not only to Christians, but to all people. If ever there was a time to deliver truth with the best we can muster, this is it. Yet today's pastors often limit themselves to talking about how to communicate better with spouses or how to get into better shape. And while these topics are important, there are life-and-death issues happening right in our culture, and the nation's churches are turning a blind eye.

For this, we deserve to be carted off in shackles for not preaching, praying, and evangelizing more fervently than ever.

Never Forget—or Have We Already?

Each September 11, the nation looks back on a tragic day in history—a day with so much sadness, shock and fear, but also one that showed the resolve and unifying spirit of America.

But how much has changed in our world since September 11, 2001?

The world is a much different place than in 2001. Unfortunately, there seems to be even more hatred toward America—and, sadder still—within America. There are still many who want to harm and kill Americans and destroy our society and our ideals, replacing freedom with fear. And this is not reserved for those outside our country. We have developed an increasingly hostile attitude toward each other, because of a variety of reasons, such as where we stand politically, what we believe about sexuality, how we view gender, and even our goals economically.

September 11 was a tragic day and a black mark on our history. But many uplifting images and stories came from that day—people helping other people, rescuing others, extending a hand regardless of color or creed, background or belief. The American spirit shone through during a terrible time. I wonder if the same spirit would show itself today. Would we have the same compassion for a stranger who believes differently than we do? If ever there was a time to unite and mirror the America we were years ago, it is now. Division in America is killing that American spirit, and only the saving redemption of Jesus Christ will ever revive it.

At the same time, however, we must stand for our beliefs in every aspect of life. Our American traditional values still matter.

The Strength of Traditional Values

Philosopher and scientist Ernst Haeckel (1834-1919) was once lecturing a group of college students and began to incorrectly address some matters of history. Recognizing that their teacher was speaking outside of his realm of expertise, a student who was a history major objected, "Professor Haeckel, the facts say otherwise." But the doctor's mind was already made up. Shrugging, he said, "So much the worse for the facts!"

Truth is not defined by popular opinion and reality is not changed by mass misconception. That appears to be the mindset of many people today regarding a number of issues. Facts, reality, and the committed pursuit of truth seem to be of minimal importance. Certainly, no issues have become more polarizing in our culture than those of sexual orientation, gender, and of course, same-sex marriage. Same-sex marriage has been celebrated by media figures, mainstreamed into daily conversation, and (as of June 2015) sanctioned by America's highest court.

Acceptance of same-sex marriage was insisted upon, and is now legally and tacitly accepted. Because the only thing weaker than the attention span of the American people is their moral awareness and resolve, very soon few will remember that there ever was objection to same-sex marriage.

But do these things make it right? Does popular will make a re-definition of marriage even possible? I am keenly aware that my answer of "no" to these questions leads some to assume my opposition to a redefinition of marriage is borne out of ignorance and homophobia. Labels like "hater" and "wingnut" are attributed to me on a regular basis because of my belief that there is an objective moral code that we would be unwise to ignore.

As a researcher who has spent well over two decades researching spiritual, moral, and cultural issues, I can say that evidence favoring what many call "traditional values" is compelling. Academically, I am persuaded of the reality of a moral law that transcends time and culture, and I am equally convinced that the Bible is true and trustworthy. As a follower of Christ, I must stand where Scripture stands, even though it may not be popular to do so. That is why I must gently remind people that truth is not defined by popular opinion and reality is not changed by mass misconception.

Repetition and savvy marketing may make gay marriage acceptable in the eyes of the public, but it will never legitimize it in the eyes of the Lord. Even so, here are a few points worth keeping in mind:

- Every person is made in God's image and, therefore, is of incredible value. This includes all people, regardless of where they land on the marriage issue.
- Everyone should respond to this issue with love and compassion, not hate.
- The Bible says what it says on the topic; we would be wise to deeply reflect on why it says what it does about moral issues.
- We need to carefully consider what history, science, and moral law say in regard to the arguments both for and against homosexuality.
- We must always remember that whatever our Christian views are on this question, they don't change the heart of the gospel

message or the evidence for it; Christ died for each of us and rose again, triumphant. This is good news!

Although I espouse a position that is not supportive of the homosexual lifestyle or gay marriage, everyone involved in this debate can be encouraged to exhibit compassion and understanding.

Let's Talk about Race

Race relations in America continues to create national conversations. In recent years, our country has been plagued with increasingly violent racial unrest, deep political divisiveness, and even spiritual brokenness among the faithful. As we prayed for ways to spur Americans to radical change, God-driven action, and world-altering steps for our recent Truth For A New Generation conference, we felt led to directly address what God's Word and history tell us on this issue. To do so, I invited my friend and African American leader Abraham Hamilton III.

At the American Family Association, Abraham Hamilton III serves as General Counsel and Public Policy Analyst. He is a husband, father of five children, lawyer, home-school dad, Bible teacher, and a nationally syndicated radio talk show host. Hamilton has an undergraduate degree in New Testament Biblical Literature from Oral Roberts University and a Juris Doctor degree from Loyola University New Orleans College of Law. He is a member of the bar associations for Louisiana, Houston and Texas, as well as the Federal Bar Association. In the legal profession, Hamilton served as a criminal prosecutor, handling major felony prosecutions at the trial level. His ministerial focuses include marriage, family, biblical worldview training, and discipleship formation. He spoke on the ground-breaking topic of "African Christianity Predates the Trans-Atlantic Slave Trade" from his unique perspective.

The focus of his talk showed Christianity's early and powerful entry into Africa. From the Day of Pentecost (Acts 2), Africans have embraced the gospel—and shared it. In the early centuries of the church, African theologians often led the way on creedal statements and controversies within the church. Even Martin Luther, the leader of the Protestant Reformation, looked to an African religious structure as his example for reforming Christianity in Europe.

Hamilton shared it was only in recent centuries that Christianity has been seen as a "white man's religion." The truth of history shows quite the opposite. As brothers and sisters in Christ—white, African American, or any other ethnicity—we ultimately find our family bond through Jesus.

His words were received with a standing ovation that night. My prayer is that what began that evening in North Carolina will spread throughout the American church as we seek to speak truth and live with love toward those of all backgrounds.

White Supremacists Have More in Common With ISIS Than Patriotism

It frustrates me that mainstream media, however, tends to portray all white Christians as white supremacists who are out to harm the world. Terms like "white privilege" and "systemic racism" are used to make an everyday American sound worse than a lone wolf inspired by ISIS. Yet if we look to the founding document of America, the Declaration of

Independence, which says that all are created equal and made in God's image, we find there is an objective moral code.

Racism in any form should be condemned. Regardless of ethnicity, America is about one race: the human race. The Christian worldview on which America was founded on says all people have value, worth, and are deserving of respect because they are made in God's image. White supremacists have more in common with ISIS than with American patriotism.

From Racism to Relativism

Planet Earth is fast becoming a "no-truth zone."[60] Relativism is the death of "true truth," or "extinction of the idea that any particular thing can be known for sure." The denial of absolute truth also has serious implications for Christianity. Today's denial of absolute truth leads to statements such as these:

- All religions lead to God.
- All religions teach basically the same thing.
- Jesus is one of many great spiritual leaders.
- No such thing as ultimate truth exists.
- All beliefs are equally valid.

Have you ever heard people make statements like these?

- "We all have our own truths..."
- "There is no moral right or wrong. Beliefs about truth and morality are based on personal situations, cultural bias, or on one's religious upbringing..."

Sadly, even some Christians believe these statements, like the young lady at the bank who told me, "We all have our own truths." This relativistic spirit presents challenges for both mission-minded Christians and values-minded Americans: How can people be convinced to turn from sin if they cannot be convinced of the true statement that they have sinned? And how can our children and grandchildren live according to biblical morals when a relativistic posture seems to be a prerequisite in social, academic, and professional arenas?

Think of the implications of this for preaching the gospel. If there is no actual, absolute truth, or if ultimate truth exists but is unknowable, then the Christian's claims about Jesus being the exclusive way to God are fallacious. Equally false (in the minds of many) are the Christians' claims that people are fallen, sinful, in need of salvation, and without Jesus Christ are bound for eternity apart from God. Surveys validate the point that when it comes to religious claims, most Americans today are driven by relativism.

Relativism has become the most prominent worldview of our times. The assumptions of relativism (at least in terms of theology) are that all beliefs are equally valid. Christianity's claim that people need Jesus Christ seems ludicrous to people who are committed to what might be described as absolute subjectivism.

When the truth dies, then so do ethics, because if nothing can be known for sure, then there are no real rights or wrongs. Combine this with self-ism, and anything goes. Relativism is—in practice—no different from having no morality at all. This explains why people can allow society to do things like kill babies and take the lives of people deemed unfit to live. According to relativism, truth has become what the majority thinks; truth is no longer based on a firm foundation; truth is whatever is right at the moment. Frederick Moore Vinson, a former chief justice of the Supreme Court said, "Nothing is more certain in modern society than the principle that there are no absolutes."[61]

What Happened to Truth?

What happened to the idea that there is one truth? How do people conclude some things are true for some people but not true for others?

The roots of this thinking reach back seven hundred years to the Renaissance. This historical period, which began in Florence, Italy, and spanned roughly four centuries from the 1300s to the late 1500s, was considered a time of rebirth. In fact, that is what *renaissance* means in French. It was not a rebirth of man, though, but of "the idea of man." It switched positions for God and man; instead of God being the measure of all things, as had been the case since the founding of Christianity, man became the measure. This was the beginning of humanism as a philosophical idea.

Francesco Petrarch (1304-1374), an Italian scholar, is considered the father of humanism. He promoted the idea of the strong, idealistic man and centered his works on man and man's ability. Renaissance humanism is "the broad concern with the study and imitation of classical antiquity which was characteristic of the period and found its expression in scholarship and education and in many other areas, including the arts and sciences."[62] This thought process developed into modern-day humanism, with its emphasis on human values and humanity in general.

The late Francis Schaeffer, a Christian scholar, wrote:

These paid men of letters translated Latin, wrote speeches, and acted as secretaries...Their humanism meant, first of all, a veneration for everything ancient and especially the writings of the Greek and Roman age. Although this past age did include the early Christian church, it became increasingly clear that the sort of human autonomy that many of the Renaissance humanists had in mind referred exclusively to the non-Christian Greco-Roman world. Thus, Renaissance humanism steadily evolved toward modern humanism—a value system rooted in the belief that man is his own measure, that man is autonomous, totally independent.[63]

Humanism showed the "victory of man." This is seen, for example, in the statue of *David*, completed in 1504 by Michelangelo. This *David* is supposed to be the David of the Bible, yet he is shown as a strong, handsome man who is obviously not Jewish because he is uncircumcised. This statue of David portrays him as the complete opposite of the young, humble David of the Bible. Most of the art of this time portrayed the same message: "Man will make himself great. Man, by himself will tear himself out of nature and free himself from it. Man will be victorious."[64]

The humanists were sure that man could solve every problem. "Man starting from himself, tearing himself out of the rock, out of nature, could solve all," Schaeffer wrote. "The humanistic cry was 'I can do what I will; just give me until tomorrow.'"[65]

Eventually, this idea failed. The optimism of the Renaissance ended in pessimism. For many centuries learned thinkers promised they would deliver the truth, and yet the truth—the truth without God, at least—remained elusive. People finally concluded that there is no truth. As modern man, whether he realizes it or not, is governed in large measure by this pessimism about truth, a philosophy called postmodernism, the belief that there are no absolutes, including no absolute truth.

According to postmodern thinking, this is the ultimate truth; people can construct their own "stories" or narratives, and what is true for one person might not be true for another. Truth is relative to individual people, times, and places. If truth is relative to each person, each person is then free to do his own thing—the perfect motto of the 1960s and 1970s. The hippies of the sixties preached peace and love, with a generous dose of drugs and illicit sex. Their main belief was, "Do your own thing. If it doesn't hurt anyone and it makes you happy, do it."

Unfortunately, many Christians bought into this worldview. The dominant ethic was to just be left alone; this was basically the attitude of apathy. Humanism, in the meantime, tried to make a comeback. The problem was that humanism had already destroyed everything it hoped to build on. According to Schaeffer, humanism—man beginning only from himself—had destroyed the old basis of truth and could find no way to generate with certainty any new truths.

In the resulting vacuum the impoverished values of personal peace and affluence had come to stand supreme. And now for many young people, after the passing of the false hopes of drugs as an ideology, the emptiness of the sexual revolution, and the failure of politics, what remained? Only apathy. Hope was gone. This was exemplified in the "whatever" culture of the past generation. Yet, as we'll see in Chapter 11, Generation Z may be returning to the focus on happiness and success. The worldview of our culture tends to spin in various cycles, yet without moral truth will remain untethered—and ultimately unsuccessful.

Instilling a love of truth in the hearts of people is more critical now than ever. The truth that truth exists must be asserted firmly but lovingly. First Thessalonians 2:4-6 and Galatians 1:10 demand that believers speak the truth! Ministers (or other Christians) are not here to tickle the ears of people. As J.P. Moreland wrote, "Saint Paul tells us that the church—not the university, the media, or the public schools—is the pillar and support of the truth (1 Timothy 3:15)."[66] Pilate asked Jesus what is perhaps the ultimate question: "What is truth?" (John 18:38).

Five facts about truth that are undeniable:

- Undeniable fact one: Truth exists.
- Undeniable fact two: Truth can be known.
- Undeniable fact three: Truth corresponds to reality.
- Undeniable fact four: Truth can be expressed in words.
- Undeniable fact five: Truth is personally relevant.

An authentic commitment to truth involves both *orthodoxy* (right belief) and *orthopraxy* (right action). A relationship with the One who called Himself *the* truth (John 14:6) must manifest itself in what one believes and how one behaves. Though some in today's culture work hard to suppress the obvious, truth *does* exist. Recognition of this within our generation must take place if our culture—and the souls of many people—are to be saved.

10

PRAY WITH GOD'S PEOPLE

Several years ago, I had the opportunity to speak at a series of meetings at a church in North Carolina. Shortly before the Sunday evening services, the pastor came to me distraught, revealing, "I've just found out my sister in Texas is in a coma and is not expected to live. I have to leave to see her."

He was upset both because of her situation as well as the fact that she had never come to faith in Jesus Christ. His sister had lived a hard life, and now she was facing death with no opportunity to hear the gospel.

That night I asked the congregation to pray for the soul of this dear woman. We bowed before God and literally begged for her recovery and a positive response to Jesus Christ. In our Monday night revival meeting, I asked the church to join me in fasting and prayer as we continued to pour out our hearts before the Lord for this dear pastor's sister. This plea extended through Tuesday as well.

On Wednesday, we received a call—God had heard our prayers.

The pastor called to report his sister had briefly revived from her coma. She called out for her brother, saying, "I'm going to die and I'm not ready!" He came, shared the gospel with his dying sister, and she prayed with him to believe in Jesus Christ.

When the news reached us, we rejoiced, but only briefly. We soon discovered his sister soon slipped back into a coma, dying twenty-four hours later.

The pastor mourned her loss, yet took joy in knowing his sister had received eternal life. The church considered it a miracle, a special intervention by God on behalf of the prayers of His people.

I'll never forget that season of prayer. We prayed as if her life depended on it—because it did. We fought on our knees for the soul of one person who had yet to trust in Jesus. We asked the Holy Spirit to act—and He did.

Our Desperate Need of the Holy Spirit Today

I'm often asked, "What should be every Christian's deepest desire?" Some mention changes in government. Others speak about the importance of family or the end of abortion in our nation. While these are important topics, God calls every believer to seek revival.

What if we took time today to pray for our nation the way a small North Carolina church prayed for the soul of one woman far from God? Would He intervene with a similar miracle? Could we expect His hand to point our families, churches, and country to a spiritual awakening?

James 5:16 (NKJV) reminds us, *"The effective, fervent prayer of a righteous man avails much."* Second Chronicles 7:14 (NKJV) adds, *"If My people who are called by My name will humble themselves, and pray and seek My face, and turn from their wicked ways, then I will hear from heaven, and will forgive their sin and heal their land."*

Despite the seemingly endless, nearly insurmountable challenges of our lives and nation, there is One whose power transcends every fear. We often look to God when all else fails, yet He calls us to lean on Him through every storm—before, during, and after. Only He can fix what is broken and He often chooses to bring forth His greatest changes in response to people who fight on their knees in prayer.

How to Pray for Revival

If we truly desire to rediscover revival, we must pray for it. But how? There is no magic formula, but there are several biblical principles we can apply.

1. Pray in Repentance

God's command to Israel continues to ring with relevance for us today: *"If My people who are called by My name humble themselves, and pray and seek My face, and turn from their wicked ways, then I will hear from heaven and will forgive their sin and heal their land"* (2 Chronicles 7:14 NKJV).

Notice the progression in this verse. First, it applies to God's people. Second, it is a command to humility. Third, there is the command to pray. Fourth, believers are to "seek" the face of God. Fifth, those who pray must "turn" or repent from sinful ways.

Those who did so in ancient Israel were promised three things: God would hear their prayers, forgive their sins, and heal their land. Though this promise was to the nation of Israel, God still hears those who humble themselves before the Lord. He promises to forgive our sins and cleanse us from all unrighteousness (1 John 1:9).

2. Pray in Community

Author R.A. Torrey realized the importance of the ancient practice of prayer in community. We can pray alone, but there is something special and unique about prayer with other committed believers. He notes:

> I can give a prescription that will bring a revival to any church or community or any city on earth. First, let a few Christians (they need not be many) get thoroughly right with God themselves. This is the prime essential. If this is not done, the rest that I am to say will come to nothing.
>
> Second, let them bind themselves together in a prayer group to pray for a revival until God opens the heavens and comes down.
>
> Third, let them put themselves at the disposal of God for Him to use as He sees fit in winning others to Christ. That is all!
>
> This is sure to bring a revival to any church or community. I have given this prescription around the world. It has been taken by many churches and many communities, and in no instance has it ever failed; and it cannot fail![67]

A study of the early church notes much of their prayer time involved time together. When we pray with other believers, there is a very real sense in which God is in our midst (Matthew 18:20).

3. Pray Continually

The first Christians were instructed, "Pray continually" (1 Thessalonians 5:17 NIV). This was the practice of the apostles and early believers in Jerusalem (Acts 2:42). To pray continually is to pray without stopping or to pray all the time. It is not praying the same words repeatedly (Matthew 6:7), but communicating with God on an ongoing, daily basis. Moses offered a strong example of this as the leader of the Jewish people, while Jesus was regularly noted as praying (Matthew 26:36; Mark 1:35; Luke 5:16). Pastor John MacArthur writes, "It is living in continual God-consciousness, where everything you see and experience becomes a kind of prayer, lived in deep awareness of and surrender to Him. It should be instant and intimate communication—not unlike that which we enjoy with our best friend."[68]

4. Pray With Priority

Many American Christians embrace the tradition of praying before eating a meal. Why? It is an opportunity to thank God for His provision. Yet we often fail to give prayer the same priority at other times. In fact, a good comparison would be to treat our prayer life the same way many people treat their smart phones. For example, many Americans look at their phones:

- First thing in the morning
- More than 100 times throughout the day
- One last time before going to sleep, and
- If they wake up at night

Consider prayer with a similar level of importance and you'll be on the right track. Try praying...

- when you first awake
- before each meal
- several times throughout the day
- during meetings with others
- before falling asleep
- when you wake up at night

When we feel like we cannot go long without prayer, we are connected with the Lord in a way that has historically preceded personal revival and national awakening.

5. Pray for Personal Awakening

Prayer is personal. If we are serious about revival, it must begin within our own hearts. Dr. Ronnie Floyd's challenging words to remind us for the need to pray for God to intervene in our personal lives as well as in our nation:

> You may have given up on America, but God hasn't. You may have given up on your church, but God hasn't. You may have given up on ministry, but God hasn't. You may have given up on yourself, but God hasn't.
>
> Our God can do anything, anytime, anywhere, with anyone. God can do more in a moment than you could ever do in a lifetime.[69]

The prophet Elijah is the last person we would expect to need spiritual awakening. However, after fleeing for his life from the evil queen Jezebel, he told the Lord, *"It is enough; now, O Lord, take away my life..."* (1 Kings 19:4 NASB). After God strengthened Elijah to continue the journey, he hid in a cave. During this dark hour, it was time alone with the Lord that encouraged Elijah to continue. After this experience, he found the power he needed for the next step of God's mission.

You may feel weak today, but God is not done with you yet. Make time to be alone with God. Tell Him how you feel. Ask for His strength to guide you. Perhaps your current situation has been uniquely designed to point you toward a fresh time with the Lord for renewed personal revival.

6. Pray for the Transformation of Others

We pray for both our own spiritual lives and the lives of others. We must believe the gospel should be shared with others with *urgency*. Too often, we say the gospel must be shared for others to know Christ and have eternal life, yet we do not live accordingly. How can we pray for those who do not know the Lord? Roger Oldham suggests the following advice:

- Ask the Lord to let you really see the people you encounter daily.
- Introduce yourself. Get their names. Create a prayer list, writing their names in a prayer journal or on a paper you keep in your Bible.
- Repeat their names in prayer each day during your quiet time.
- Address them by name as you see them along the way, getting to know more about them each time you see them.

- Mention to them that you recently prayed for them.
- Ask them how you might pray for them.
- Continue to lift them up in prayer.
- Do not become discouraged if they do not quickly confess faith in Jesus Christ.
- Take note, when the Lord sees your passion for the lost, He will bring others into your path who are longing to be saved![70]

7. Pray With Expectation

James is clear our prayers must be bold. We do not pray in doubt; we pray with expectation: *"But let him ask in faith, with no doubting, for the one who doubts is like a wave of the sea that is driven and tossed by the wind. For that person must not suppose that he will receive anything from the Lord; he is a double-minded man, unstable in all his ways"* (James 1:6-8 NKJV).

Jesus provided a similar teaching in Mark 11:23 (ESV): *"Truly, I say to you, whoever says to this mountain, 'Be taken up and thrown into the sea,' and does not doubt in his heart, but believes that what he says will come to pass, it will be done for him."* We are called to live by faith and pray by faith, expecting God to work in mighty ways.

Flickers of Spiritual Awakening

These principles are not only aspirations, they are becoming reality. As I've traveled the nation to speak to congregations, I have a growing sense God is on the verge of bringing revival to His people. In fact, my home state of North Carolina has once experienced such revival in an unexpected way.

On Mother's Day 2016, New Hope Baptist Church began a one-week revival featuring evangelist C.T. Townsend. Near the end of the week, pastor Randy Hobbs sensed God was leading them to continue meeting. They continued to meet each night, soon outgrowing the church sanctuary.

A large tent was set up on a local property and attendance continued to grow. Person after person came to faith in Jesus, while believers repented of sins. Soon more than 2,500 people attended each night. At a youth night in June, more than 5,000 people, mostly teenagers, came to hear the gospel.

None of these events made national news, but God was up to something. Pastor Randy noted, "It's just amazing to be a part of this. This is something we've been praying for in our church for several years.... We had been meeting over 15 years, praying for revival to touch us locally and nationally."[71]

Could God's work in Burlington be the small beginnings of a larger movement of awakening in America? What would happen if you and those in your local church began to urgently pray together for God to awaken your community? We cannot create revival, but we can pray for it. We dare not manufacture awakening, but we can long for it.

Let's face today's cultural challenges with bold prayer, seeking God's best for the future of our land and our lives. God is not done with you yet—or our nation. We each have a role to play to help our nation rediscover revival.

11

PREPARE YOUR HEART

Philosopher Friedrich Nietzsche said, "All philosophy falls forfeit to history." As news headlines continue to change moment-by-moment, I am amazed at the similarities between America in 2020 and Germany in the late 1930s. There are at least five ways the stability of our nation is being undermined.

Are these trends a coincidence? Is it simply the consequences of our hedonistic culture? Are powerful elitists manipulating world events to usher in a new world order? I won't speculate on this aspect here, but I do want to clearly state some issues that are not speculation. These five trends are happening now, in real time, and unless some modicum of basic order and lawfulness is reintroduced, our Constitution and country are in danger. Our nation's stability is more fragile than we realize.

Social Disorder

The first issue is social disorder. We've already discussed the ongoing and increasing riots and revolutions in the streets of America. New York

City recently agreed to defund its police force to the tune of $1 billion![72] What do New Yorkers expect police to do? Will they stop robberies with social workers or offers of free education? I don't think so! The result will not be a more peaceful city, but more likely the need for state and federal defense to fill the gap. We may soon see the National Guard as the norm in the streets of New York City, moving the nation one step closer to the harsh military controls of Nazi Germany.

Revised History

HBO Max recently decided to remove the 1939 classic film *Gone with the Wind* from its network, citing its "ethnic and racial prejudices." Never mind that the film led to Hattie McDaniel becoming the first black American to win an Oscar. Just find history you don't agree with in 2020 and hit "delete."

The level of revisionist history in our nation has become so ridiculous as to border on satire. The well-known BabylonBee.com even clapped back at recent revisionism with its headline, "Liberals Heroically Prevent History From Repeating Itself By Removing All References to History."[73] No longer content with learning from the past, the left continues to methodically remove the past.

Famous films of yesterday are certainly not the only target. Who would have guessed *American* activists would destroy national monuments and statues from our nation's history? Christopher Columbus has turned from hero to zero with Antifa and similar groups who have targeted his statues in Minneapolis, Boston, Richmond, and Miami. The takedown in

Miami included spray painting George Floyd's name on the base of the statue, as if that justified the action.

Who knew there would be a day when the President of the United States would find it necessary to sign an executive order to protect statues from its own citizens? Let's be clear. This is not activism; this is vandalism. In our nation, when someone has a dispute, there are legal ways to implement change. Destruction of property is not a legal option. Yet liberals somehow embrace the let's-do-wrong-to-create-right mentality that has historically led to socialism and worse—including signs resembling what led to Hitler's rise in Germany.

Leveraged Language

As the pick-your-gender-of-the-day movement began its acceleration across America in 2016, University of Michigan student Grant Strobl provided a perfect example of why it's not a good idea to let students choose their own preferred pronouns. When asked by his professor which pronoun he preferred, Grant chose "His Majesty."[74] I love that! If we are going to allow students to choose any fantasyland identity they wish, why not go big? Grant used the title to highlight the absurdity of allowing people to choose identity. Even as a college student, he realized gender is not something we create or choose, but it is part of how we are created as humans.

In 2020, leftists claim pronouns like "he" or "she," or "Mr." and "Mrs." are "heterosexist." Some argue phrases like "God bless America" are "hate speech." Liberals are changing the language to change the story. However, language serves as a vital foundation of society. Without clearly defined language, our Constitution becomes meaningless. We've already become a nation largely based on case law rather than Constitutional Law. The increase in leverage language increasingly turns traditional terms into hate speech, much like the volatile changes in language used to fuel anti-Semitism in Nazi Germany.

Controlled News

There was a day when the three major networks each broadcast the same basic news events with slight variations. Today, I can watch the same event unfold on two different networks and wonder if we are even talking about the same event!

For example, on July 4, 2020, FoxNews.com led with a story of President Trump honoring Justice Scalia, Jackie Robinson, and others in a new National Garden for American heroes. On the same day, CNN.com provided a lead headline reading "Trump tries to drag America backward on a very different July 4th." Are we talking about the same person on the same day about the same events? Journalism is no longer even attempting objectivity. Instead, the bias of each station clearly promotes its own worldview each day, while millions of viewers glibly drink it in without realizing the poison they consume.

One of America's great freedoms has been freedom of the press. While we can produce any content we would like, the controlling media networks of our culture largely lean—and even fall—left, controlling news more than any other time in modern American history.

Censorship

America was once the land of the free and the home of the brave. It is increasingly the land of the censored and the home of cancel culture. Twitter no longer allows political advertising of any kind. However, defining "political" content is often a nebulous term. Facebook, which also owns Instagram, Messenger, and WhatsApp, has ramped up its censorship through AI-based filters and partnerships with left-leaning "fact checking" organizations. Anyone who even types, "A man is not a woman and a woman is not a man," is now no longer safe on social media.

Much more could be noted, but these five areas point toward an America that more closely resembles Nazi Germany prior to World War II than the America of 1776. As some American cities teeter on the brink of anarchy, this violence and instability makes us very vulnerable for irrevocable change—and not for the better. Again, the famed philosopher Friedrich Nietzsche said, "All philosophy falls forfeit to history." What did he mean by this? Well, his point was that philosophies and predictions about the future give way to history. In other words, what *actually* happens.

Liberal progressivism philosophized that welfare, moral relativism, and socialism would give us some type of utopia. I well remember public education in the 1970s, in which "new math" discouraged teachers from ever telling students that an answer was "wrong." Critical thinking skills and logic have been replaced by quests for self-esteem and unrestricted self-expression. As we look at these five trends dismantling our nation, I have to ask about this philosophy of, "No rules but my rules," and "No truth but my own truth," how's that working for you?

Slogans and Truth

Are slogans the same thing as truth? Are we believing and living on truth, or are we accepting and repeating vacuous slogans? I was online recently and a viewer of my program asked me what I thought about some of the recent happenings in the aftermath of George Floyd's tragic murder. The email asks what I, as a minister and Christian leader, plan to do about, "the most racist organization in America...*the church.*"

He began his email in all caps, urging me, "DON'T ACT LIKE YOU DON'T KNOW...Don't act like you don't see it...the church is systemically racist." He jabbed about, "...the overwhelming depiction of Jesus as a white man..."

However, when I asked him for specifics about where or when I or other Christians have insisted Jesus is a white man, I was given no evidence. While I am quick to emphatically say the death of George Floyd was wrong and that racism is sinful, it does not mean Christ and the teachings of Christianity are racist. In contrast, the church also demonstrably does many virtuous things in our society. How many of today's hospitals, soup kitchens, literacy programs, and other social services were started by Christians? Undeniably, most of the beneficial social programs in today's American communities have historically been started by followers of Jesus.

In contrast, I've yet to visit a developing nation and come across a well provided by American Atheists. I've never been in an inner city homeless shelter funded by Norman Lear's People United for the Separation of Church and State. However, when I responded to the man who emailed me on this issue, he abruptly replied with personal attacks claiming I was "being a jerk" for stating historical facts about Christianity.

We are trading the pursuit of truth for the shouting of slogans. We are losing the rule of law for a state of disorder. While self-appointed social justice "warriors" repeat slogans that feel good and draw mainstream media attention, it is imperative that we stand on the solid foundations of truth and reality without continued freefall into a politically correct fantasyland.

Mobs can rip down historical statues, spray paint slogans in giant letters on our public streets, censor 80-year-old movies that offend them, ban books that don't suit their "narrative," label facts they don't like as "hate speech," terrorize American patriots with violence, and muzzle people so that they can no longer exercise *their* right to free speech, but that doesn't make their "truth" true.

If leftists try to truly "defund" police, remove civil liberties to quarantine Americans indefinitely, and tell Christians they cannot sing praises to God in their own churches, they are in for a rude awakening. The gospel cannot be quarantined! God's people cannot be silenced by the eradication of law and order, or even by eradicating the police. Individual liberties cannot forever be suppressed, and people can't forever be quarantined and controlled.

A few years ago, a trend called "The Blasphemy Challenge" became popular online.[75] The challenge was an Internet-related activity that encouraged people to post a clip of themselves cursing God. The more brazen clips include assertions that the person willingly accepts the consequences this action (including hell) incurs should it turn out that God *does* exist.

Blasphemy-challenge promoters made no secret of their desire to promote atheism among teens. One website offered to send a free DVD documentary against Christianity to teens who posted a video rejection of God. One of the project's organizers told Fox News, "It (the blasphemy challenge) exposes the crock that is Christian doctrine."

Online atheists based their so-called "blasphemy challenge" on Scriptures such as Mark 3:29 (ESV) in which Jesus says, *"But whoever blasphemes against the Holy Spirit will never be forgiven; he is guilty of an eternal sin."* Based on this Scripture, some atheists fault God for apparently being unable or unwilling to forgive this specific sin.

But what exactly is blasphemy? Are there unforgivable or unpardonable sins? How does a person know whether they have "crossed the line" and passed beyond the point of God's forgiveness?

Biblical examples of blasphemy imply irreverence or slander against God. But the term also means "to spurn." The Scriptures alluding to "blasphemy against the Holy Spirit" imply a two-fold indictment against the leaders who personally encountered Jesus while He was here on Earth. They refused to acknowledge Jesus as the Messiah, *plus* they accused Him of being empowered by Satan. To say the least, they *spurned* Jesus.

Most scholars agree that Jesus' ominous warnings about "blaspheming the Holy Spirit" represent a situation unique to the time that Christ was on Earth. However, such trends among young people should be concerning, especially since the taunts of blasphemy-challenge videos are directed almost exclusively at the God of Christianity.

The rise of spiritual skepticism and outright blasphemy are vivid reminders that Christians must strive to live out their faith. After listing the spiritual qualities that ought to be tangibly present in a Christian's life, Galatians 5:23 says that "against such things there is no law." In other words, it can't be argued against. The blasphemy of an unbelieving world is tangibly answered by a testimony of Christ-likeness on the part of God's people.

From Blaspheming God to Believers of Discouragement

A discouraged minister recently told me, "At one time I thought that I was going to help change the world. Now that the years have gone by, I realize that it's just not possible to make much of a difference. You get by, and maybe leave a mark here or there." He seemed disappointed and very jaded. This once-energetic leader exhibited spiritual and emotional "battle fatigue."

However, it is important to also recognize the encouraging aspects we have in our nation. In addition to our many national freedoms, Jesus provided a hard-won victory on the cross that offers us five spiritual liberties no one can take away:

1. Freedom from guilt that all inherit

The Bible says in 1 Corinthians 15:22 (NIV), "In Adam all die." Physical death and the risk of spiritual death are universal realities because of the sin we inherit from Adam and Eve. In Christ we are forgiven, promised a home in heaven, and are set free from guilt.

2. Freedom from wrong deeds we personally commit

We have all known the right but have done the wrong. Wrongful actions not only put a wedge between us and God, they result in numerable negative repercussions. Christ forgives our sins, and the indwelling Holy Spirit can give us the strength to overcome temptations.

3. Freedom within ourselves over personal struggles

If we are willing, God's Spirit can even help us overcome sinful habits that may have held us in bondage for years. Whether the issue is a gnawing remorse over past bad decisions, feelings of worthlessness, emotional pain from abuse, or just fear about tomorrow, Jesus gives us peace within. The gospel is our way to peace with God, and is also the key to peace with ourselves.

4. Freedom from judgment that is ultimately coming

Jesus is in the process of restoring a broken world. "Eschatology" is the word theologians use to refer to what the Bible says about "last things." One day the entire world and universe will be made brand-new (Revelation 21:5). Just as there is a global, universal eschatology, Jesus gives us a joyous personal eschatology. This fallen world is under judgment, but Jesus has made the believer exempt!

5. Freedom to face eternity, and our soul's final destiny

Hebrews 9:27 (HCSB) says, *"It is appointed for people to die once—and after this, judgment."* We may not want to think about our own mortality, but it is unavoidable. There is a date that we will leave this world, and God knows when that date is. It is very freeing to know that we are ready to face God!

In His Heart a Man Plans His Course...

We often forget that finding God's will isn't a guarantee of monetary success or prosperity. Nor does it mean life will be blissfully trouble free. It has been said Christianity is not the subtraction of all problems but the addition of God's presence in every problem.

Also, God's will doesn't come to us like a downloadable file of meticulously drawn plans. Many mature Christians counsel against the assumption that God has one single, fixed, cut-and-dried set of blueprints for each believer's life. Within God's boundaries for moral living and basic Christian growth, a believer may sincerely make a variety of choices and remain in "God's will."

Yes, arriving at God's will isn't like cracking a secret code or needing a precise combination of ingredients for a recipe. It is a relationship based on abiding in Christ in every circumstance. Many people care most about some goal or "end result," but God desires that they walk with Him daily through the process.

...But the Lord Determines His Steps

God's will for people in general is that they be saved (1 Timothy 2:3-4). He patiently beckons to people because He's not willing that any should perish (2 Peter 3:9). Some things commanded by God are specific to Christians, such as reading and following Scripture (1 Timothy 4:13), prayer (Luke 18:1; 1 Timothy 2:1-2), corporate worship (Hebrews 10:25), and evangelism (Acts 1:8). Christians are to maintain an attitude of thankfulness (1 Thessalonians 5:18), and are to faithfully handle their lives before God (1 Corinthians 6:19-20).

The clearest biblical information about God's will for believers is that they live morally pure (1 Thessalonians 4:3; 1 Peter 4:2). What is God's will? That I live a Christ-honoring life based on biblical truth. But within those guidelines, Christians have liberty (John 8:36; 1 Corinthians 10:23).

No person needs to be paralyzed by fear of making a wrong move that irrevocably sets him or her on a devastating course. The believer in Christ truly is free. This isn't to say we can rely solely on guesses or gut feelings. God directs us through His Word, prayer, promptings of the Holy Spirit, circumstances, and other people. Other influential variables include our personal desires and talents and common sense.

Over time, a person can cultivate the ability to make angst-free decisions. We may sometimes be keenly aware of what God wants us to do. Other times, God may stretch us as we progress purely on faith. God's will is often discovered gradually and seen most clearly in retrospect. Scripture promises to direct the paths of faithful disciples (Proverbs 3:5-6) and give believers abundant life (John 10:10). But believers should be confident because, even greater than knowing God's will, they have the privilege of knowing God.

The Battle Is Not Finished Yet

Not long ago I was asked to visit the friend of a friend who had been arrested and put in jail. As a minister of the gospel, requests like this come along more than you might imagine. It is an honor to do such things, and when people find themselves in the deepest of valleys they are very often quite open to allowing Jesus Christ to become Lord of their life.

The facility was very bleak, with rough gray concrete everywhere and seemingly endless hallways of bars and flaking paint. Not surprisingly, an air of gloom and hopelessness permeated the place, and this was reflected on the faces of the inmates.

The jail where I visited the inmate in question had a very small court-yard in the middle of the building. There were a few concrete squares in an otherwise dirt courtyard. The dusty courtyard area reminded me of forlorn places I have been in developing nations. Suddenly I noticed a small flower growing up against the concrete wall in one corner. It was the only bit of vegetation in this otherwise lifeless place. Invisibly, some breeze had carried a grain of pollen over the roof and into this small open area within the prison facility. The bleakness of the surroundings made that one little flower even more vivid.

When you think of the bondage, sufferings, and entanglements that permeate this world, the freedoms that we have through Christ appear even more precious. Jesus is the flower of beauty in a barren, dusty place. He absolves the guilty who are imprisoned by sin. The heart longs for freedom, and finds it in Christ.

No one is immune to discouragement, but it is easy to feel burdened by the deplorable condition of our culture. Deep down inside, we would all like to make a difference in the world. At the risk of sounding naive—and at the risk of being criticized for wishful thinking—I challenge to you admit it: Wouldn't you like to make a positive difference in the world—if you could?

You may have asked yourself, "Can't *anybody* do something about the condition of our world? Can't someone help make America better?"

There is a person who can be used to radically improve things in today's world. There is a person who, if they chose to do so, could make an impact that would have eternal implications.

Let's face it—the only type of person who could make a difference in this world, the only type of person who could stand up and address the challenges we face today, would have to be a person led by God Almighty. But I'm not talking about some great evangelist or pastor. There *is* a person God can use to change the world, and we desperately need this person to step up and accept the challenge of making a difference for God. How serious is the need for dedication on the part of this person?

Spiritual awakening and cultural change could be influenced by what this person does. The souls of people are at stake, futures hang in the balance. The eternal destiny of specific individuals could be changed forever if this person would rise to face the spiritual challenges of the hour. There is such a person with potential to make an eternal difference for Christ, for truth, and for the good.

Maybe the person of whom I am speaking is unaware that they have the potential for such widespread transformation. The individual I'm talking about, poised to shake our culture, holding the key to a better future, is you.

Your response may be, "Me? Change the world?" My answer is, "Absolutely!" Do you love Christ, believe the Scriptures, and care about what is right? Are you one of the remnant whose heart is characterized by obedience to Jesus and compassion for the souls of people? If so, you are poised and positioned, ready to be used by God to alter eternity.

In times of crisis, God raises up leaders. Israel faced many situations of genuine danger, times when their nation's very survival was in question. The aged Mordecai realized his relative Esther had the potential, through

God, to change their world. He challenged her, *"For if you remain completely silent at this time, relief and deliverance for the Jews will arrive from another place, but you and your father's house will perish. Yet who knows whether you have come to the kingdom for such a time as this?"* (Esther 4:14 NKJV).

Like Esther, your life situation at this moment is not an accident. God can work through you in unimaginable ways for incalculable good—if you are willing to be used. We need spiritual power to overcome America's fatal flaw. You have a role in bringing this about! Let's consider three aspects regarding your part in bringing about authentic impact in America.

You Have a Personal Role in Changing America

In an interview with Fox News, I noted that younger generations are filled with hope. Millennials and Generation Z have a heart to serve others. I used to struggle to recruit young people for a mission trip. Today, service and volunteering are central values of young people.

But when it comes to other areas of spiritual growth, many American teens believe in a combination of works-righteousness, religion as psychological well-being, but a distant non-interfering God. It's almost as if they believe God is a benign therapist and He exists to enhance my life experience but He certainly wouldn't interfere with my life.

Overall, however, one of the greatest contributors to broken faith among young people stems from broken families. We may not be able to change every person in our nation, but we can take responsibility to start with changing the citizens in our own home.

You can make a positive, tangible difference that will have eternal implications. History's great revivals feature stories of God using individuals. Do away with the "somebody else" attitude! That "somebody else" God wants to use to change our society is you. You will be the one to challenge the school board. You will be the one who helps end abortions in your community. You will be the one who helps our veterans find respect in our society. You will be the one to teach the next generation the great story of God at work in our nation.

Allow me to let you in on a secret: "Somebody else" doesn't exist! God will work in your life when you see that putting your faith in action is your responsibility. It is also your privilege. "Somebody else" can't walk with Jesus for you. You must do it yourself. You must know Christ personally, stand for the gospel openly, and understand hope will not be realized if we wait for "somebody else" to initiate it.

It is almost as if we are wishing that the evils in this world will be addressed by somebody more spiritual and more courageous than ourselves! America's awakening will come when everyday, ordinary, God-loving citizens see themselves as personally accountable for the spiritual future of the nation.

You Have a Unique Destiny to Fulfill in God's Purpose

If you are a person of God, the possibility of you being a "world changer" should not strike you as surprising! Jesus said, *"Truly, truly, I say to you, whoever believes in me will also do the works that I do; and greater works than these will he do, because I am going to the Father. Whatever you ask in my name, this I will do, that the Father may be glorified in the Son"* (John 14:12-13 ESV).

Those who love God cannot passively watch from the sidelines, unable to make a difference in this world of spiritual need! After Jesus' ascension to heaven, the Holy Spirit came in *power* to the church to *empower* the church! God has made it possible for every child of God to make a tangible difference in the world!

Without exception, every born-again Christian has spiritual gifts divinely imparted by God for the building up of His kingdom. Are you using your abilities for God's purposes? The Bible reminds us to not let our "tools" get rusty! "Therefore, I remind you to stir up the gift of God which is in you..." (2 Timothy 1:6 NKJV). Your community, church, and country need you *now*. If your heart is still beating and you are still breathing, God has you here for a purpose. Are you living with purpose today?

God Will Empower You to Fulfill Your Destiny

It is unfortunate that many in our society choose to rely on their own strength and believe "the power is within you." Those who know God realize that He is God—not us. In our own strength, we can do nothing. No man or woman can hope to change this world for eternity. Only God can do it. But God works through people! The person surrendered to God can be used by God to fulfill the purposes of God.

God wants to empower you, but He is not sending you on a solo mission. We cannot hope to overcome America's fatal flaw in our own limited strength. But through the Holy Spirit's power, God can use you to accomplish great purposes. It has been said that most of our limits are self-imposed. How true! Despite your past or physical limitations, God can use you, and He will! But remember Jesus' words, *"without Me you can do nothing"* (John 15:5 NKJV).

The Destiny You Must Fulfill

The world needs God; the church needs revival. It is doubtful that any honest American would argue these points. But realize that even though these calls are monumental in scope, God has historically acted to address these needs by working through people like you.

Let me ask: Do you speak the truth even when it is not popular? Do you express your Christian faith to others? Are you courageous enough to remind people that, "The Bible says that there is no salvation apart from Jesus Christ" (Acts 4:12)? Are you willing to obediently speak the truths people need to hear, though they may not be what people want to hear?

Renewal has come when some God-empowered individuals dared to challenge the status quo. Change has always been initiated when a humble servant of God has squared off against the prevailing thought of the day. You, like Esther, have an option. You can take a stand for what you believe, regardless of the cost. You can initiate deliverance from what would otherwise be a time of destruction. Like Esther, and countless faithful leaders of the past, you can rise to the challenge of our day and do the right thing so you, your family, and our nation may not perish.

12

WHY ELECTIONS AND ISSUES STILL MATTER

An interesting name picked up traction during the last presidential cycle. Trump supporters (and conservatives in general) were nicknamed with the moniker "Deplorables." The term caught on, with my friend and radio host Todd Starnes even publishing a book called *The Deplorables' Guide to Making America Great Again.* (A great read, by the way.)

During that time, I participated in a radio interview for a liberal Washington, DC, talk show. A listener called in with what I hoped would be a genuine question. Instead, I heard the words, "Burn in hell, maggot."[76]

During my interview, I tried to defend the fact that this nation was based on the Ten Commandments and godly principles, citing facts that are part of our nation's rich history.

I have debated hundreds of leading leftists, and frankly, pleaded with them for their very souls.

The liberal host, an atheist, responded with sarcasm and contempt at every mention I made about God or morality. When I said that the Supreme Court was wrong to redefine marriage (which goes against

2,000 years of Western civilization, not to mention our own national moral foundation), the host accused me of calling for lynchings and the killing of LGBT people.

I have learned in hundreds of media interviews with leftist journalists, as well as interactions with the academic elites of the left, that they—like former presidential candidate Hillary Clinton—truly believe people of faith are "deplorable." Deep down, they find the idea of God and morality deplorable.

The notion that we are accountable to a moral law and the reality that we will one day give account for our actions and face a holy God is met with scorn and derision. Hillary Clinton believes Christians and moral people are deplorable, because we are reminding the left of something they really don't want to think about—God, the ultimate Moral One.

I've spent more than 20 years speaking on college campuses and giving media interviews. I have been part of countless debates over the years that question God's existence. When the cameras stop rolling, many people look me in the eye, searching, and ask, "Is God real?" But in front of the camera, or the classroom and courtroom, the fight against God rages on.

Pastors, religious leaders, and churches help restore the moral and Christian fabric of our nation. The left is trying to abolish what they find deplorable—God. But when America has been sanitized of speech and people deemed "unfit" and "deplorable," who, along with God and morality, will be "dealt with"?

You and me. People of faith. Conservatives. I have talked with and debated many leading leftists, and frankly, pleaded with them for their own souls. Some are honest enough to admit their desire for God and to talk with me about their spiritual questions. But most, in their desire to legitimize things that deep down they know are wrong, dig in their heels for the fight against God. And the target they are firing at most are people of faith—people of values, churches, pastors in their pulpits, religious schools, soup kitchens, and ministries led by Protestants and Catholics. You know, all of us "deplorable" people.

Why the Actions of We, the Deplorables, Matter

Why do elections still matter? Many issues could be mentioned, but one of fundamental importance to every American is our national security.[77] King David, called a man after God's own heart in Acts 13:22, was also a man of war. God did not allow David to construct the Temple in Jerusalem, leaving that task for his son, Solomon—whose hands had never known bloodshed.

We can interpret this in a variety of ways. Does this mean God views military activity as something intrinsically wrong? Did God view the blood that David shed as a stain that irrevocably defiled his religious worship? If so, what might this mean for a Christian's views about national security?

Any leader who denies the danger from radical Islamist terrorists is not making the people's safety a priority and should not have a place in office. Our nation was founded on biblical ethics. Many today dispute this, but John Marshall (the first chief justice of the U.S. Supreme Court) wrote in 1833: "The American population is entirely Christian, and with us Christianity and Religion are identified. It would be strange indeed, if with such a people, our institutions did not presuppose Christianity, and did not often refer to it, and exhibit relations to it."

Some question how maintaining a strong military reconciles with Christ's admonition to "love thy neighbor." But in wrestling with this, consider several undeniable realities of the 21ˢᵗ century—more nations than ever before have access to nuclear weapons. The world has become an increasingly violent place, and world news is dominated by endless acts of terrorism. The Christian moral code that shaped and civilized the Western world has been all but discarded.

Unsettling to think about, but this is truth.

What should be America's commitment to national defense? And what about the question of Christians encouraging a strong national defense, serving in the military or becoming a law enforcement officer? If a government operates with a Christian moral code in view, it is permissible—even honorable—for a Christian to serve as a police officer or as a soldier. Further, military weakness in this fallen world is simply not a realistic position. It actually opens the door to greater evils.

President Theodore Roosevelt was a devout Christian; after leaving office, he turned down college presidencies to spend several years self-publishing a Christian newspaper. In 1905, he said, "There could be no greater calamity than for free peoples, the enlightened, independent, and peace-loving peoples, to disarm while yet leaving it open to any barbarism or despotism to remain armed." Belief in a strong national defense is not only biblical—it is mature, responsible, and morally right.

Roosevelt arguably presided over a much safer world than we do, yet in his day he lobbied for a strong military because "the world is as unorganized as now." Because of their biblical and moral underpinnings, Roosevelt believed that America and the West alone could secure for the rest of the world "a just peace."

After the election of Donald Trump, many wondered what will our next president do to shore up national security? What will our commander-in-chief do about immigration policies that have undermined the safety of U.S. citizens? In recent years, the Immigration and Naturalization Service (at the behest of the White House) has opened the borders to tens of thousands of refugees with ties to terrorism—dumping these people (who are sometimes dangerous) in heartland communities, and in a very unorganized fashion.

In 2016, a chief of police in a mid-sized American city gravely explained to me that over the last four years, authorities had uncovered and intercepted more than 100 terrorist plots designed to be carried out locally. So here is the question: How committed will our next president be to make sure that we are not subjected to another 9/11?

That the U.S. is a benevolent, compassionate, philanthropic nation is not in question. But a commitment to bettering the human condition does not mandate that national security be compromised in the process—nor the welfare and wishes of American voters be ignored.

Let's be realistic. Terrorism exists, and for a leader of our country not to acknowledge this fact or pretend that these threats are a thing of the past puts the American people at risk. Any leader who denies that danger, including from radical Islamist terrorists, is not making the people's safety a priority and should not have a place in office—nor does that leader deserve our vote.

Military initiatives exist because of the pervasive presence of evil in the world, which itself is a result of the human propensity for sin. Christians should remember, though, that their King has already fought the most important battle. Jesus, through His death on the cross, triumphed over His enemies (Colossians 2:14).

When Jesus returns, He will fully consummate His victory and His kingdom, making all things new (Revelation 21–22). There will then be no need for human government, a standing army—nor for local police forces. But until the Prince of Peace returns, it is honorable and biblical for Christians to stand for the "greater good" by supporting that which promotes the "common good"—peace officers, a just military, and civil authority. Electing candidates who believe in a strong national defense is not only biblical, it is mature, responsible, and morally right.

Transgenderism and National Defense

In a similar way, as the media and Internet collectively melt down over President Donald Trump's seeking to ban from the military those who struggle with gender confusion, the president may be about a higher purpose than he realizes. So much more than sexual accommodation within the military, or within the culture at large, is at stake. The mainstreaming of homosexuality, the redefinition of marriage, the eisegesis of rights into the Constitution where inalienable rights previously would never have been implied—none of these social and political machinations could be implemented unless a pesky (for the left, anyway) little problem were forced out of the way: natural law.[78]

Great thinkers throughout history, religious and philosophical leaders, not to mention the framers of our nation, have called it by many names: self-evident truth, objective morality, undeniable truth, and "natural law." Space does not permit delineation of all implied by natural law, but for the purposes of this book, let me point out three things natural law would tell us:

1. Males and females are different. People of every era and culture know this.

2. One's gender is an inherent and unalterable part of what it means to be a human being.

3. These things come from and are tied to God.

Since the 1960s, our culture has been at war with natural law. We know deep inside that killing babies is wrong, for example. But to legalize abortion and not feel guilty about it, we've spent decades engaging in mental gymnastics, denying that life begins at conception and quibbling over when a human fetus should be recognized as a person.

Regarding the long-term conditioning of public consciousness so that homosexuality is gradually accepted—or at least, over time, made to appear less counter-intuitive—our children are fed junk science and junk history. Historical revisionism, to spin opposition to natural law in a positive light, has birthed a cottage industry of what could only be called "anti-knowledge." (In a couple of debates I have done, pro-LGBTQ academics have said to me, "Throughout history, the nature of marriage has always been fluid." This is simply false.)

But to usher in the moral and social changes that progressives and leftists envision, natural law must be abolished. Or at least *recognition* of natural law must be abolished. The problem is, you can't abolish what is part of the DNA of reality. Alexander Hamilton, whose influence on the creation and understanding of the Constitution can hardly be overstated, spoke often of "natural law" and God, and of our obligation to acknowledge both. Hamilton called this moral law "eternal and immutable law" and stated that it is "obligatory upon all mankind, prior to any human institution whatever. This is what is called the law of nature...Upon this law depend the natural rights of mankind."

Because of our desire to legitimize behaviors we know are wrong, humans ignore natural law or try to deny an awareness of it. But Hamilton and the Founders believed in human accountability to natural law, because in our consciousness and in nature, God has inexorably revealed moral truth. Hamilton said, "The sacred lights of mankind...can never be erased or obscured by mortal power. No tribunal, no codes, no systems can repeal or impair this law of God, for by His eternal law, it is inherent in the nature of things."

In jettisoning natural law and God, from whom it emanates, we are positioning ourselves for a very bleak future. And we are paving the way for a hell on earth for our children's children. One of two futures await America and the West in the absence of a recovery of moral truth and natural law: either the iron fist of communism or the iron sword of Sharia. Only the affirmation of natural law and morality, and government based thereon, are sufficient to hold those two forces at bay.

The framers of the Constitution understood that if we recognize God's weaving of natural law and objective morality into the fabric of life, we could experience a blessed "manifest destiny." Should these things not be recovered, we will continue to head toward inevitable tragedy. In mandating that our military not capitulate to the transgender lobby, the president scored a point for the defense of natural law.

If support for natural law is restored, President Trump will have done more than strengthen our military, he may ultimately contribute to the saving of America.

Eight Questions That Show Elections Still Matter

Although a growing number of Americans are choosing to "walk away" from the polls and neglect conservative issues altogether, this pivotal time in America's history is too important for any citizen to turn away.

Christian voters, pastors, and churches have a huge stake in the outcome. Not voting means not only throwing away our privilege and duty to vote, but also essentially casting a vote for someone who may do more harm to the country than good. We each have both the biblical and the civil responsibility to not only vote but to take our values, and some serious considerations, to the polls with us.

As we face elections, whether local or presidential, the following is a list of eight considerations for those who seek to support candidates who support godly values and constitutional government:

1. Remember that "the perfect is the enemy of the good."

God can use any presidential candidate for His purpose; all candidates are flawed. Will we allow these flaws, which we all have, to make us cast a protest vote or not vote at all?

2. Will my life be better or worse under this president?

When people were given this line to fill in before the last presidential election—"My outlook on the culture as a whole compared to 10 years ago is..."—about 96 percent reported they felt "worse" about the culture, with the remaining reporting they felt "better" or "the same."

3. Will this president protect my religious freedom?

What are the candidates' plans for preserving the religious liberties on which the country was founded, especially as more and more freedoms are being taken away?

4. How will this candidate protect life?

Abortion, euthanasia, and other life matters have historically been important issues for voters. While the Republican platform is one of the most pro-life in the party's history, the Democratic platform asserts that a woman has the right to abort her unborn child, a black mark on the nation since Roe v. Wade in 1973.

5. Will this candidate protect our country?

The safety and defense of the country is of paramount importance. National security and recognition of those who seek to harm America must be a priority for our elected officials.

6. Who will these leaders agree upon for the Supreme Court?

Appointments to the court have longstanding impact, one of the most important considerations of the election. Within his first two years as President, Donald Trump had the opportunity and responsibility to appoint two Justices—decisions that will influence our nation for years to come.

7. Will this elected official protect the financial resources with which God has entrusted us?

Many people continue to struggle in today's economy, and many policies could be enacted to ease the financial burden on Americans. All human beings long to have the dignity that comes with providing for their family.

8. Will I feel good about the decisions this political leader will make?

Overall, will I still be glad that I voted the way I did in 10 years? And, more importantly, did I carefully consider my vote in prayer?

Our recent midterm elections have once again revealed the importance of choosing candidates that support our American values. When Americans voice their vote in ways that encourage patriotism and constitutional government, the aspirations of our Founders continue to find fulfillment today.

SOMETHING ONLY YOU CAN DO

Today, people are quarantined; one day, evil and suffering will be. Can we trust that God is with us during a pandemic? Does all the pain, social upheaval, and desperation indicate the Lord has abandoned us? Many wonder, *Where is God in the midst of all this sickness and trouble?*

Headlines struggle to adequately describe the magnitude of the coronavirus situation. COVID19-related statistics are continually being updated as accounts of death, damage, and turmoil dominate the news.

Whether facing a human-initiated tragedy like 9/11, or in times of natural disaster like recent tornados across the Southern states of our country—and now amid the chaos that is COVID19—we invariably ask ourselves, "Why?" In the process of enduring such calamities, people may wonder, *Where is God? Could He have prevented this? Does what I am going through matter to God?*

As limited, finite human beings, no one can *fully* know why a given event might have happened, or why seemingly innocent individuals suffer. But we long for an answer to the elusive issue of *why*. People in Jesus' time wanted to know why a certain man was born blind (John 9) and why lives were lost through a prominent disaster of that era (Luke 13). Should we automatically conclude that sinners were getting their "just deserts"? Or like John the Baptist's moment of doubt while in prison, should we conclude that maybe God isn't as authentic or faithful as we had first thought (Matthew 11)?

We may not know every reason behind the events of life, but meaning and hope can come from reflecting on what humans *do* know about God and this world. In a number of ways (through creation, conscience, Scripture, and through Christ Himself), God has shown His creatures that He exists. This alone is encouraging to ponder: *God has tangibly revealed Himself to humanity.* Not only may we know about God, we may personally know Him.

God has revealed much about this world and His plans for it. The Bible informs us that the original creation was perfect, but sin was introduced through human rebellion. Moral evil resulted in natural calamities (the flood of Noah, climate changes, and global weather patterns as the ripple effect of humankind's choices). Even birth defects, cancers, and viruses are among the toxins that reverberate throughout this prodigal planet.

Hope or consolation would be nonexistent if the human story ended there. However, there is valid reason to trust God's promise that He will one day "make all things new" (Revelation 21:5). John the Baptist was encouraged to evaluate his own doubts in light of the promises of Scripture and the person of Christ. Divine love, forgiveness, healing, and even victory over death are not just pious platitudes, but are realities promised by the Bible. Christ's historically verified empty tomb is tangible proof that this death-conquering Jesus was indeed in a position to authoritatively speak about the here *and* the hereafter.

Christians do not deny the realities of evil and tragedy, but we do affirm God can (and will) bring good from them. Like Jesus, we weep with those who weep (John 11:35 and Romans 12:15) and long for the day that evil will be quarantined, and this world made new. Believers everywhere extend their prayers, love, sympathy, and support for the people worldwide suffering from the coronavirus.

Our hearts are also with those suffering from the financial implications of the global pandemic. As a pastor myself, I encourage churches everywhere to help your neighbors in every way possible. Further, let us continue to pray for our president, his cabinet, for medical professionals, for first responders, and other essential workers, all valiantly serving in the shadow of this pandemic.

May God use this time to draw us all closer to each other, and closer to our heavenly Father. With a benevolent God presiding over all things, there truly is no need to panic or be fearful. At this time and always, may God enable America to pull together with brave and grateful hearts.[79]

1. Emma Green, "Why Is It Hard for Liberals to Talk about 'Family Values'?" *The Atlantic*, July 30, 2013; https://www.theatlantic.com/politics/archive/2013/07/why-is-it-hard-for-liberals-to-talk-about-family-values/278151, accessed July 24, 2020.

2. Ibid.

3. Matt Walsh, *Church of Cowards: A Wake-Up Call to Complacent Christians* (Washington: Regnery Gateway, 2020), 2-3.

4. Theodore Roosevelt, *The Works of Theodore Roosevelt* (C. Scribner's Sons, 1924), 415.

5. Opinion by Hugh Raffles, June 25, 2020; highlighted at https://www.cnn.com/2020/06/25/opinions/removing-teddy-roosevelt-statue-beginning-raffles/index.html, accessed July 24, 2020.

6. From Martin Luther King Jr.'s book, *Why We Can't Wait*, as cited at https://www.jameswatkins.com/articles-2/heavy/mlk, accessed July 24, 2020.

7.   Francis Grimke, "Equality of Rights for All Citizens, Black and White Alike," in Alice Dunbar (ed.), *Masterpieces of Negro Eloquence* (New York, 1970), 349-350.

8.   Abraham Lincoln, in *The New Encyclopedia of Christian Quotations*, comp. Mark Water (Grand Rapids: Baker Books, 2000), 764.

9.   Jessica Martinez and Gregory A. Smith, "How the faithful voted: A preliminary 2016 analysis," Pew Research Center, November 9, 2016; http://www.pewresearch.org/fact-tank/2016/11/09/how-the -faithful-voted-a-preliminary-2016-analysis/, accessed July 24, 2020.

10.   Reid Wilson, "New report finds that voter turnout in 2016 topped 2012," *The Hill*, March 16, 2017; http://thehill.com/homenews/ state-watch/324206-new-report-finds-that-voter-turnout-in -2016-topped-2012, accessed July 24, 2020.

11.   James McWilliams, "The Miracle of Trump: Why Did Evangelicals Deliver the Votes for a Sinner?" *Pacific Standard*, February 13, 2017; https://psmag.com/news/the-miracle-of-trump-why-did -evangelicals-deliver-the-votes-for-a-sinner, accessed July 24, 2020.

12.   Theodore Schleifer and Noah Gray, "30,000 turn out for Trump's Alabama pep rally," *CNN*, August 21, 2015; https://www.cnn .com/2015/08/21/politics/donald-trump-rally-mobile-alabama/ index.html, accessed July 24, 2020.

13.   Maureen Groppe, "First year of Trump-Pence brings bountiful blessing, religious conservatives say," *USA Today*, January 19, 2018; https://www.usatoday.com/story/news/politics/2018/01/19/ first-year-trump-pence-brings-bountiful-blessings-religious -conservatives-say/1044308001/, accessed July 24, 2020.

14. Michael Blechman, "Liberalism Isn't What It Used to Be," *Wall Street Journal,* June 21, 2019, A15.

15. Ibid.

16. Ibid.

17. James Madison, "The Federalist No. 51," *The Federalist* (New York: Modern Library), 337.

18. From https://ocasio2018.com/issues as of July 18, 2018.

19. Scott Rae, *Moral Choices: An Introduction to Ethics* (Grand Rapids: Zondervan, 2009), 132-38.

20. "North Carolina: To Boycott Or Not"; April 24, 2016; https://www.npr.org/2016/04/24/475512005/north-carolina-to-boycott-or-not, accessed July 24, 2020.

21. "The facts on mass shootings, guns in the United States," *PolitiFact,* May 18, 2018; http://www.politifact.com/truth-o-meter /article/2018/may/18/facts-mass-shootings-guns-united-states/, accessed July 24, 2020.

22. John Malcolm, "3 Common Traits of School Shooters," *Heritage Foundation*, March 26, 2018; https://www.heritage.org /education/commentary/3-common-traits-school-shooters, accessed July 24, 2020.

23. Ibid.

24. Find out more about Keith Deltano's work to stop bullying at www.dontbullyonline.com.

25. Andrea Peyser, "School-approved smut," *New York Post*, October 18, 2013; https://nypost.com/2013/10/18/school-approved -smut/, accessed July 24, 2020.

26. Nicholas Tampio, "Betsy DeVos said Common Core was 'dead'—it's not," *The Conversation*, March 26, 2018; https:// theconversation.com/betsy-devos-said-common-core-was-dead -its-not-92800; accessed July 27, 2020.

27. Adapted from my article "An Opportunity to Make a Difference for Christ," *Decision Magazine*, June 1, 2017; https:// decisionmagazine.com/opportunity-make-difference-christ, accessed July 24, 2020.

28. John Wesley, quoted in: *Christian History, Issue 28, Volume IX, No. 4,* 1990, page 60.

29. Will Durant, quoted in *Chicago Sun-Times,* August 24, 1975, 1B.

30. "Letter of Edward Winslow, 11 December 1621," MayflowerHistory.com; http://mayflowerhistory.com/letter -winslow-1621, accessed July 24, 2020.

31. Elizabeth M. Economou, "Look How Many College Kids Can't Speak Freely on Campus," *Lifezette*, March 13, 2018; https://www .lifezette.com/2018/03/look-how-many-college-kids-cant-speak -freely-on-campus/, accessed July 24, 2020.

32. Jeffrey M. Jones, "More U.S. College Students Say Campus Climate Deters Speech," *Gallup*, March 12, 2018; https://news. gallup.com/poll/229085/college-students-say-campus-climate- deters-speech.aspx?utm_source=tagrss&utm_medium=rss&utm_ campaign=syndication, accessed July 24, 2020.

33. "Family Research Council Statement on D. James Kennedy Ministries' Lawsuit Against the Southern Poverty Law Center," August 24, 2017; https://markets.businessinsider.com/news/stocks/family-research-council-statement-on-d-james-kennedy-ministries-lawsuit-against-the-southern-poverty-law-center-1002280189#, accessed July 24, 2020.

34. This section adapted from my article at Alex McFarland, "America, the Bloody: Reaping the Fruits of Our Abolition of Christianity," *CNS News*, July 27, 2016; https://www.cnsnews.com/commentary/alex-mcfarland/america-bloody-reaping-fruits-our-abolition-christianity, accessed July 24, 2020.

35. Todd Starnes, "No More Prayers on the Football Field!" *Lifezette*, August 25, 2017; https://www.lifezette.com/2017/08/no-more-prayers-on-football-field/, accessed July 24, 2020.

36. Edmund Kozak, "Christian Florist Faces Ruin After Losing Religious Liberty Case," *Lifezette*, February 17, 2017; https://www.lifezette.com/2017/02/christian-florist-faces-ruin-after-losing-religious-liberty-case/, accessed July 24, 2020.

37. Nicole Russell, "Twitter Permanently Bans Feminist for Writing That 'Men Aren't Women,'" *The Federalist,* November 25, 2018; https://thefederalist.com/2018/11/25/twitter-permanently-bans-feminist-writing-men-arent-women, accessed July 24, 2020.

38. Ibid.

39. Ibid.

40. Ibid.

41. Ibid.

42. Samuel Smith, "Twitter Bans 'deadnaming,' 'misgendering' trans-identified persons in updated 'hateful conduct' policy," *Christian Post*, November 28, 2018; https://www.christianpost.com/news/ twitter-bans-deadnaming-misgendering-trans-identified-persons -hateful-conduct-policy.html, accessed July 24, 2020.

43. Nicole Russell, "Twitter Permanently Bans Feminist for Writing That 'Men Aren't Women,'" *The Federalist,* November 25, 2018; https://thefederalist.com/2018/11/25/twitter-permanently-bans -feminist-writing-men-arent-women, accessed July 24, 2020.

44. John Wesley, as quoted in Donald W. Dayton's, *Discovering an Evangelical Heritage* (Peabody, Massachusetts: Hendrickson Publishers, 1992), 123.

45. "Statement by Vice President Mike Pence on Leaving Cols Game after Players Disrespect Flag and National Anthem," October 8, 2017; https://www.whitehouse.gov/briefings-statements/ statement-vice-president-mike-pence-leaving-colts-game-players -disrespect-flag-national-anthem, accessed July 24, 2020.

46. Matthew Fowler and Vladimir E. Medenica, "This is what millennials think about NFL protests," *The Washington Post*, October 5, 2017; https://www.washingtonpost.com/news/ monkey-cage/wp/2017/10/05/what-do-millennials-think -about-the-nfl-protests-our-new-survey-shows-that-varies-a-lot-by -race/?utm_term=.6dd5852aacda, accessed July 24, 2020.

47. Tyler Tynes, "Why a team of 8-year-old football players decided to kneel for the national anthem," *SBNation*, September 20, 2017; https://www.sbnation.com/2017/9/20/16338926/national -anthem-protests-st-louis-youth-football, accessed July 24, 2020.

48. From http://www.7culturalmountains.org/; accessed July 27, 2020 .

49. Adelle M. Banks, "What Americans Say About Sexual Freedom vs. Religious Liberty," *Lifezette*, July 1, 2017; https://www.lifezette .com/2017/07/what-americans-say-sexual-freedom-religious -liberty/; assessed July 24,2020.

50. "What Makes America Great?" *Barna Group*, July 3, 2017; https://www.barna.com/research/makes-america-great/, accessed July 24, 2020.

51. Ibid.

52. "Supreme Court to hear case of baker's refusal to make wedding cake for same sex couple," *Fox News*, June 26, 2017; http://www .foxnews.com/politics/2017/06/26/supreme-court-to-hear -case-bakers-refusal-to-make-wedding-cake-for-gay-couple.html, accessed July 24, 2020.

53. Adapted from my article Alex McFarland, "Why Profanity Is Wrong," *AFA Journal*, February 2014, https://afajournal .org/2014/February/022014x_language.html, accessed July 24, 2020.

54. "The New York Times/CBS News Poll on U.S. Race Relations," *New York Times*, May 4, 2015; https://www.nytimes.com/ interactive/2015/05/05/us/05poll-doc.html, accessed July 24, 2020.

55. Grace Chen, "Bringing the Bible Back to School: A Revival?" *Public School Review*, June 29, 2018, updated August 6, 2018; https://www.publicschoolreview.com/blog/bringing-the-bible-back-to-school-a-revival, accessed July 24, 2020.

56. Adapted from my article Alex McFarland, "Higher Education: 'A Four-Year Attack on God and America," February 7, 2017; https://www.lifezette.com/2017/02/higher-education-four-year-attack-america-god/, accessed July 24, 2020.

57. E. Michael Rusten and Sharon O. Rusten, *The Complete Book of When and Where in the Bible and Throughout History* (Wheaton, IL: Tyndale, 2005), 105.

58. Donald W. Dayton, *Discovering an Evangelical Heritage* (Peabody, MA: Hendrickson, 1992), 25.

59. Dennis Quinn, "Few U.S. sermons mention abortion, though discussion varies by religious affiliation and congregation size," *Pew Research,* April 29, 2020; https://www.pewresearch.org/fact-tank/2020/04/29/few-u-s-sermons-mention-abortion-though-discussion-varies-by-religious-affiliation-and-congregation-size/, accessed July 27, 2020.

60. This section adapted from my article Alex McFarland, "Responding to Relativism: Confronting the Predominant Worldview of Our Times," *The Truth Project;* https://sites.google.com/site/worldviewaddress/experimental-3/relativism/response-to-relativism, accessed July 24, 2020.

61. *Dennis v. United States*, 341 U.S. 494, 508 (1951).

62. Paul Kristeler, "Humanism," in *The Cambridge History of Renaissance Philosophy*, edited by C. Schmitt, and Q. Skinner (Cambridge: Cambridge University Press, 1988), 113.

63. Francis A. Schaeffer, *How Should We Then Live?* (Wheaton, IL: Crossway, 2005), digital edition.

64. Ibid., 71.

65. Ibid.

66. J.P. Moreland, *Love the Lord with All Your Mind* (Colorado Springs, CO: NavPress, 1997), 188.

67. R.A. Torrey, "The Christian Workers Manual, Volume 18," 1917, *Moody Bible Institute,* p. 22; https://books.google.com/books?id=XlkxAQAAMAAJ&printsec=frontcover#v=onepage&q&f=false; accessed July 27, 2020.

68. John MacArthur, *Alone with God* (Colorado Springs, CO: David C. Cook, 2011), 15-16.

69. Ronnie Floyd, "The Stakes Are High: 2016 Presidential Address to the Southern Baptist Convention," June 17, 2016; https://blog.ronniefloyd.com/date/2016/06/page/3/, accessed July 24, 2020.

70. Roger S. Oldham, "The Primacy of Prayer in Spiritual Awakening," *Baptist Press*, January 7, 2013; http://www.bpnews.net/43596; accessed July 24, 2020.

71. Mark Martin, "NC Revival Keeps Going Strong," *CBN News*, June 27, 2016; http://www1.cbn.com/cbnnews/us/2016/june/nc-revival-draws-thousands-to-burlington-and-god-rsquo-s-word, accessed July 24, 2020.

72. N'dea Yancey-Bragg, "New York City will take $1 billion from police budget, but many say it doesn't go far enough," *USA Today*, July 1, 2020; https://www.usatoday.com/story/news/nation/2020/07/01/new-york-city-budget-billion-nypd-defund-police/5354307002, accessed July 24, 2020.

73. "Liberals Heroically Prevent History From Repeating Itself By Removing All References To History," June 26, 2020; https://babylonbee.com/news/man-heroically-prevents-history-from-repeating-itself-by-removing-all-references-to-history, accessed July 24, 2020.

74. Lindsey Bever, "Students were told to select their pronouns. One chose 'His Majesty' to protest 'absurdity,'" *Washington Post*, October 7, 2016; https://www.washingtonpost.com/news/education/wp/2016/10/07/a-university-told-students-to-select-their-gender-pronouns-one-chose-his-majesty, accessed July 24, 2020.

75. Story adapted from Alex McFarland, "'The Blasphemy Challenge' Tempts Teens to Curse God," *CharismaNews.com,* September 22, 2014; https://www.charismanews.com/opinion/45236-the-blasphemy-challenge-tempts-teens-to-curse-god, accessed July 24, 2020.

76. Adapted from my article Alex McFarland, "People of Faith Are 'Deplorable' to the Left," *Lifezette*, September 23, 2016; https://www.lifezette.com/2016/09/people-faith-are-deplorable-to-left/, accessed July 24, 2020.

77. This section adapted from my article "The Christian Perspective on National Security," *Lifezette*, September 20, 2016; https://www .lifezette.com/2016/09/the-christian-perspective-on-national -security/, accessed July 24, 2020.

78. Adapted from my article Alex McFarland, "How Trump's Transgender Military Ban May Help America Preserve Natural Law," *Lifezette*, August 4, 2017; https://www.lifezette. com/2017/08/how-trump-transgender-military-ban-help -america-preserve-natural-law/, accessed July 24, 2020.

79. Adapted from my article Alex McFarland, "Today, people are quarantined; One day, evil and suffering will be," March 30, 2020; https://www.truthpr.com/today-people-are-quarantined-one-day -evil-and-suffering-will-be/, accessed July 24, 2020.

HOW TO BEGIN
A RELATIONSHIP
WITH GOD

People everywhere invest their lives in the search for meaning, purpose, and fulfillment. But people need something more than money, fame, luxurious houses, good looks, nice cars, or a lucrative stock portfolio. There is nothing necessarily wrong with these things, but they cannot provide peace to the soul or forgiveness of one's sin.

I once read that the highest rates of suicide and divorce occur among the most affluent classes of society. On the West Coast of the U.S., psychologists and counselors have isolated a new affliction and have given it a name, "Sudden Acquired Wealth Syndrome." People are achieving every benchmark that our society says should make them happy, but they are finding that it is possible to be materially rich, yet spiritually bankrupt. Many people have a schedule that is full, but a heart that is empty.

Several years ago, our 9-member ministry team crossed America on a 50-States-in-50-Days trip. During this journey to 50 states in 50 days,

I preached in every service, in all 50 U.S. states, and personally talked with thousands of people. We had the privilege of hosting 64 worship services, throughout the entire U.S. Our outreach team met many people who came to us with probing questions and genuine concern about spiritual issues. People today truly are looking for meaningful answers, craving hope in a dangerous world.

Present realities, such as worldwide terrorist attacks, global economic uncertainty, political instability, and natural disasters like hurricane Katrina have only intensified this search.

Immediately after the terrorist attacks of 9/11, I went to New York City to help with a prayer center that had been set up by the Billy Graham ministry and Samaritan's Purse. Just like on my 50-state tour, I was talking daily to hundreds of people from every background imaginable. They may have expressed themselves in different ways, but they all had the same basic question: *"Who is God, and how may I come to know Him?"*

Where one stands with God is the most vital of all issues, but the good news is that you may settle this today! You may have wondered, *How does a person become a Christian? How can I be certain that my sin is forgiven? How may I experience consistent spiritual growth?* Let's consider these things together.

God's Word Explains the Message of Salvation

Jesus says in John 3:3 (NKJV), *"Unless one is born again, he cannot see the kingdom of God."* Salvation is the issue: The most important question you will ever ask yourself is this: Do I know for certain that I have eternal life, and that I will go to heaven when I die?

If you stood before God right now, and God asked, "Why should I let you into My heaven?" what would you say?

The Bible describes our condition: *"For all have sinned, and fall short of the glory of God"* (Romans 3:23 NKJV). Just as a job pays a wage at the end of the week, our sins will yield a result at the end of a lifetime: *"For the wages of sin is death* [the Bible describes this as separation from God, the punishment of hell], *but the gift of God is eternal life, in Christ Jesus our Lord"* (Romans 6:23).

God's love for you personally is shown by His provision for your need: *"But God demonstrates His love toward us, in that while we were still sinners, Christ died for us"* (Romans 5:8 NKJV).

Salvation requires repentance, which means a "turning." Jesus said, *"Unless you repent, you will all likewise perish"* (Luke 13:3 NKJV). The New Testament emphasizes the necessity of repentance and salvation: *"Repent therefore and be converted, that your sins may be blotted out"* (Acts 3:19 NKJV).

Every one of us has sinned, and the Bible says that our sins must be dealt with. We have a twofold sin problem. We are sinners by birth, and we are sinners by choice. Someone once spoke with the great evangelist Dr. Vance Havner, "This thing about man's sin nature, I find that hard to swallow!" Dr. Havner said, "You don't have to swallow it—you're born with it, it's already in you."

The world classifies sin, viewing some things as worse than others. But the Bible teaches that all sin is an offense against God, and even one sin is serious enough to keep someone out of heaven. You may not have robbed a bank, or maybe you have. God doesn't grade on a curve; humanity is a tainted race, and sin is the problem.

Oftentimes in life, we know what is right, but we do what is wrong. You may have even looked back at yourself and wondered, *What was I thinking? Why did I do that? How could I have said that?* Jesus said that people need to repent, and make a change. Repentance means turning *from* your sins, and *to* Christ. By faith, trust *who* Jesus is (God's Son; mankind's Savior), and *what* Jesus did (died in your place, and rose from the dead).

God's forgiveness is received by faith. We are to confess our faith before others, not ashamed to let the world know that we believe in Jesus: *"That if you confess with your mouth the Lord Jesus and believe in your heart that God has raised Him from the dead, you will be saved. For with the heart one believes to righteousness, and with the mouth confession is made unto salvation"* (Romans 10:9-10 NKJV).

What is faith? Faith is trust. It is simple, honest, childlike trust. God says that you have a sin problem, but that He loves you, and will forgive you. God says that through Jesus Christ, He has made a way for anyone to be saved who will come to Him. Do you trust what God has said, and what God has done? If you come to Christ in belief and faith, God promises to save you: *"For whoever calls on the name of the Lord shall be saved"* (Romans 10:13 NKJV). Jesus promises: *"...the one who comes to Me, I will by no means cast out"* (John 6:37 NKJV).

During the 50-state tour, we gave away thousands of yellow stickers with the words, *"Jesus Saves, Pray Today!"* That is not a trite saying, or marketing cliché. It is a deep biblical truth; and if you desire to have a relationship with the Lord, that can be accomplished right where you are now. Make your journey to the cross today through saying this basic prayer of commitment:

"Dear Lord Jesus, I know that I have sinned, and I cannot save myself. I believe that You are the Son of God, and that You died and rose again for me, to forgive my sins, and to be my Savior. I turn from my sins, and I ask You to forgive me. I receive You into my heart as my Lord and Savior. Jesus, thank You for saving me now. Help me to live the rest of my life for You. Amen."

God's Word Gives You Assurance of Salvation

You can overcome doubts about where you stand with God. Based on what God's Word says—not what you feel or assume—you can know that you have eternal life: *"He who has the Son has life.... These things have I written to you who believe in the name of the Son of God, that you may know that you have eternal life..."* (1 John 5:12-13 NKJV).

Jesus said, *"He who hears My word and believes in Him who sent Me has everlasting life, and shall not come into judgment, but has passed from death into life"* (John 5:24). Remember, you are not saved by good works, and you are not "kept saved" by good works. Your merit before God is totally based on Jesus; His perfection, holiness, and righteousness is credited to each one who believes by faith.

What Is Meant by the Term "Re-Dedication?"

A news reporter once asked me this question. He had heard me use this term as I spoke at a church, and wanted to know what I meant. "Rededication" is for a believer who desires that their walk with Christ be renewed and deepened. A Christian can wander from God in sin, or simply lose their closeness to the Lord through the busyness of life.

A born-again Christian is forever God's child. Your salvation is a matter of *"sonship."* Your daily Christian growth is a matter of *"fellowship."* Your spiritual birth into God's family is in some ways, similar to your physical birth into the human family. For instance, in growing up as a child, you may have disobeyed and disappointed your father. Something you did may have grieved your father, but you were still his child, because you had been born into that family.

In the same way, the Christian's relationship to the Lord is still intact, even though a sin we commit may hinder our daily fellowship with God. Salvation is a one-time, instantaneous event; Christian growth, and personal fellowship with God is an everyday, lifelong process. Consistent daily prayer, Bible study, obedience to the Holy Spirit, and nurture in a local church fellowship are all keys to growth and Christian maturity.

While your "sonship" may be intact, your daily "fellowship" may be lacking. Christ, not "self" must be on the throne of your heart and life! Sin hinders our fellowship with God. *"But your iniquities have separated between you from your God; and your sins have hidden His face from you, so that He will not hear"* (Isaiah 59:2 NKJV). Perhaps your desire is like that of David, when he had wandered from God, *"Create in me a clean heart, O God, and renew a steadfast spirit within me"* (Psalm 51:10 NKJV).

God lovingly receives all who *turn* to Him, and all who *return* to Him! He cleanses us from sin and restores us to fellowship with Him. King David had been "a man after God's own heart," but his sinful deeds required that he humbly re-commit himself to the Lord: *"Do not cast me away from Your presence...restore to me the joy of Your salvation"* (Psalm 51:11-12). Christian publications often use the following verse in the context of evangelism, and that is okay, but 1 John 1:9 is really a promise to the *Christian* who needs to make things right with the Lord: *"If we confess our sins, He is faithful and just to forgive us our sins, and to cleanse us from all unrighteousness."*

From the same chapter is another great truth that gives us precious, sweet assurance: *"But if we walk in the light, as He is in the light, we have fellowship one with another, and the blood of Jesus Christ His Son cleanses us from all sin"* (1 John 1:7 NKJV).

You may already know the Lord, but wish to pray these basic words of re-dedication and commitment:

"Lord Jesus, I acknowledge that I have sinned and wandered from You. I confess my sin, and turn from it. I recommit myself to You as Lord. Thank You for forgiving me; I trust You to give me the strength to live for You each day of my life. Thank You for being my Savior, my Lord, and my Friend. Amen."

May God bless you, as you journey on with Him.

If you made a decision for Christ just now, it would be an honor to hear from you. If you do not have a Bible and would like to request one, or if you have other questions or spiritual needs, write to:

Dr. Alex McFarland

c/o Truth for a New Generation

PO Box 10231

Greensboro, NC 27404

Or email us through the website at alexmcfarland.com.

NATIONAL MOTTO,
DECLARATION OF INDEPENDENCE, AND A CALL TO PROCLAIM THEM

Historical documents, writings, and records—for use in classrooms—censorship of which in public school classrooms is generally forbidden. Teachers and administrators in local schools are generally open to assemblies being hosted by outside presenters, especially when

a) the speaker has the endorsement/support of vocal parents and trusted faculty members;

b) the subject matter is relevant to existing curriculum, is especially relevant to current events, or is of significant educational value;

c) students themselves request the speaker to come.

The future status of public school assemblies (or of school attendance in general) in this age of COVID and the quarantines is unknown. One way that conservative/Christian speakers are able to legally make presentations on campuses is through *clubs*. Most middle and high schools have clubs that meet either before school starts or in the afternoon once classes have ended.

Legally, if a public school has *any* student clubs (chess club, diversity club, philosophy club, 4-H club, etc.) then Christian clubs must also be allowed—provided that the clubs are student led, have at least one faculty sponsor, and that attendance (by other students) is voluntary. It has been my honor to speak in more than 200 public schools, both in student-led clubs and in school-wide assemblies.

One may share much of the gospel message and the basics of a biblical worldview merely by quoting America's Founders. Speakers who are willing to patiently work to gain an invitation to a school may present vital truths about our nation's history—and I know from experience that students are eager to hear, and will express much gratitude that you have come to enrich them with this important content.

Students realize that the uplifting facts about our history have not been presented to them; even very young students seem to intuitively grasp that America's "God and country" legacy is very important for them to know about.

Content to which all public school students—and their teachers—should be exposed, includes:

1. National Motto

2. National Anthem

3. Pledge of Allegiance

4. Declaration of Independence

5. U.S. Constitution

6. State charter (all 50 state charters are worth reading; most mention God and/or morality)

7. Writings, speeches, documents, and proclamations of America's Founders and of U.S. Presidents

Note: Legally, censorship of these readings may not legally be done merely because so much of the historical record contains religious content. There are a number of Christian and pro-conservative legal societies in the U.S. willing to assist when students and educators are victims of one of the left's most insidious tactics, that of *viewpoint discrimination.*

The United States National Motto

"In God We Trust"; adopted by 84th the U.S. Congress (P.L. 84–851); signed into law by President Eisenhower on July 30, 1956.

The Declaration of Independence

IN CONGRESS, July 4, 1776.

The unanimous Declaration of the thirteen united States of America,

When in the Course of human events, it becomes necessary for one people to dissolve the political bands which have connected them with another, and to assume among the powers of the earth, the separate and equal station to which the Laws of Nature and of Nature's God entitle them, a decent respect to the opinions of mankind requires that they should declare the causes which impel them to the separation.

We hold these truths to be self-evident, that all men are created equal, that they are endowed by their Creator with certain unalienable Rights, that among these are Life, Liberty and the pursuit of Happiness.–That to secure these rights, Governments are instituted among Men, deriving their just powers from the consent of the governed, –That whenever any Form of Government becomes destructive of these ends, it is the Right of the People to alter or to abolish it, and to institute new Government, laying its foundation on such principles and organizing its powers in such form, as to them shall seem most likely to effect their Safety and Happiness. Prudence, indeed, will dictate that Governments long established should not be changed for light and transient causes; and accordingly all experience hath shewn, that mankind are more disposed to suffer, while evils are sufferable, than to right themselves by abolishing the forms to which they are accustomed. But when a long train of abuses and usurpations, pursuing invariably the same Object evinces a design to reduce them under absolute Despotism, it is their right, it is their duty, to throw off such Government, and to provide new Guards for their future security.–Such has been the patient sufferance of these Colonies; and such is now the necessity which constrains them to alter their former Systems of Government. The history of the present King of Great Britain is a history of repeated injuries and usurpations, all having in direct object the establishment of an absolute Tyranny over these States. To prove this, let Facts be submitted to a candid world.

He has refused his Assent to Laws, the most wholesome and necessary for the public good.

He has forbidden his Governors to pass Laws of immediate and pressing importance, unless suspended in their operation till his Assent should be obtained; and when so suspended, he has utterly neglected to attend to them.

He has refused to pass other Laws for the accommodation of large districts of people, unless those people would relinquish the right of Representation in the Legislature, a right inestimable to them and formidable to tyrants only.

He has called together legislative bodies at places unusual, uncomfortable, and distant from the depository of their public Records, for the sole purpose of fatiguing them into compliance with his measures.

He has dissolved Representative Houses repeatedly, for opposing with manly firmness his invasions on the rights of the people.

He has refused for a long time, after such dissolutions, to cause others to be elected; whereby the Legislative powers, incapable of Annihilation, have returned to the People at large for their exercise; the State remaining in the mean time exposed to all the dangers of invasion from without, and convulsions within.

He has endeavoured to prevent the population of these States; for that purpose obstructing the Laws for Naturalization of Foreigners; refusing to pass others to encourage their migrations hither, and raising the conditions of new Appropriations of Lands.

He has obstructed the Administration of Justice, by refusing his Assent to Laws for establishing Judiciary powers.

He has made Judges dependent on his Will alone, for the tenure of their offices, and the amount and payment of their salaries.

He has erected a multitude of New Offices, and sent hither swarms of Officers to harrass our people, and eat out their substance.

He has kept among us, in times of peace, Standing Armies without the Consent of our legislatures.

He has affected to render the Military independent of and superior to the Civil power.

He has combined with others to subject us to a jurisdiction foreign to our constitution, and unacknowledged by our laws; giving his Assent to their Acts of pretended Legislation:

For Quartering large bodies of armed troops among us:

For protecting them, by a mock Trial, from punishment for any Murders which they should commit on the Inhabitants of these States:

For cutting off our Trade with all parts of the world:

For imposing Taxes on us without our Consent:

For depriving us in many cases, of the benefits of Trial by Jury:

For transporting us beyond Seas to be tried for pretended offences

For abolishing the free System of English Laws in a neighbouring Province, establishing therein an Arbitrary government, and enlarging its Boundaries so as to render it at once an example and fit instrument for introducing the same absolute rule into these Colonies:

For taking away our Charters, abolishing our most valuable Laws, and altering fundamentally the Forms of our Governments:

For suspending our own Legislatures, and declaring themselves invested with power to legislate for us in all cases whatsoever.

He has abdicated Government here, by declaring us out of his Protection and waging War against us.

He has plundered our seas, ravaged our Coasts, burnt our towns, and destroyed the lives of our people.

He is at this time transporting large Armies of foreign Mercenaries to compleat the works of death, desolation and tyranny, already begun with circumstances of Cruelty & perfidy scarcely paralleled in the most barbarous ages, and totally unworthy the Head of a civilized nation.

He has constrained our fellow Citizens taken Captive on the high Seas to bear Arms against their Country, to become the executioners of their friends and Brethren, or to fall themselves by their Hands.

He has excited domestic insurrections amongst us, and has endeavoured to bring on the inhabitants of our frontiers, the merciless Indian Savages, whose known rule of warfare, is an undistinguished destruction of all ages, sexes and conditions.

In every stage of these Oppressions We have Petitioned for Redress in the most humble terms: Our repeated Petitions have been answered only by repeated injury. A Prince whose character is thus marked by every act which may define a Tyrant, is unfit to be the ruler of a free people.

Nor have We been wanting in attentions to our Brittish brethren. We have warned them from time to time of attempts by their legislature to extend an unwarrantable jurisdiction over us. We have reminded them of the circumstances of our emigration and settlement here. We have appealed to their native justice and magnanimity, and we have conjured them by the ties of our common kindred to disavow these usurpations, which, would inevitably interrupt our connections and correspondence. They too have been deaf to the voice of justice and of consanguinity. We must, therefore, acquiesce in the necessity, which denounces our Separation, and hold them, as we hold the rest of mankind, Enemies in War, in Peace Friends.

We, therefore, the Representatives of the united States of America, in General Congress, Assembled, appealing to the Supreme Judge of the world for the rectitude of our intentions, do, in the Name, and by Authority of the good People of these Colonies, solemnly publish and declare, That these United Colonies are, and of Right ought to be Free and Independent States; that they are Absolved from all Allegiance to the British Crown, and that all political connection between them and the State of Great Britain, is and ought to be totally dissolved; and that as Free and Independent States, they have full Power to levy War, conclude Peace, contract Alliances, establish Commerce, and to do all other Acts and Things which Independent States may of right do. And for the support of this Declaration, with a firm reliance on the protection of divine Providence, we mutually pledge to each other our Lives, our Fortunes and our sacred Honor.

ADDITIONAL SOURCES AND RECOMMENDED READING

T*hose who read, lead."* This quote has been attributed to several notables. While its original source is unknown to me, the truth of this observation is clear. Each reader is strongly encouraged to build a library for themselves that will, ultimately, shape you for a lifetime.

The following is a list of books relevant to the issues presented here. Of course, by no means exhaustive, this very limited list is provided to encourage further study of America's miraculous history and tenuous present. The author and publisher pray that this book and ones such as listed will inspire and mobilize people in every state to stand strong for the preservation of our country.

Barton, David. *Original Intent: The Courts, the Constitution, and Religion.* Aledo, Texas: Wallbuilders Press, 2008.

Barton, David. *Setting the Record Straight: American History in Black & White*. Aledo, Texas: Wallbuilders Press, 2004.

Beliles, Mark A., and Newcombe, Jerry. *Doubting Thomas? The Religious Life and Legacy of Thomas Jefferson*. New York: Morgan James, 2015.

Connell, Janice T. *Faith of Our Founding Father: The Spiritual Journey of George Washington*. New York: Hatherleigh Press, 2004.

Dayton, Donald W. *Discovering an Evangelical Heritage*. Peabody, Massachusetts: Hendrickson Publishers, 1992.

Dershowitz, Alan, ed. *The Federalist Papers*. New York: Skyhorse Publishing, 2019.

Eberstadt, Mary. *How the West Really Lost God*. West Conshohocken, Pennsylvania: Templeton Press, 2013.

Erickson, Erick, and Bill Blankschaen. *You Will Be Made to Care: The War on Faith, Family, and Your Freedom to Believe*. Washington, DC: Regnery, 2016.

Federer, William J. *America's God and Country Encyclopedia of Quotations*. Coppel, Texas: Frame Publishing, 1996.

Federer, William J. *Prayers and Presidents*. St. Louis, Missouri: AmeriSearch, 2010.

Fisher, Dan. *Bringing Back the Black Robed Regiment*. Mustang, Oklahoma: Tate Publishing, 2015.

Goldman, David P. *How Civilizations Die.* Washington, DC: Regnery Publishing, 2011.

Hagedorn, Thomas W. *Founding Zealots, How Evangelicals Created America's First Public Schools, 1783-1865.* Cincinnati, Ohio: Christian History In America, 2013.

Hall, Verna. *The Christian History of the Constitution of the United States of America.* San Francisco: Foundation for American Christian Education, 1966.

Hart, Benjamin. *Faith and Freedom: The Christian Roots of American Liberty.* San Bernardino: Here's Life Publishers, 1988.

Harte, John. *How Churchill Saved Civilization.* New York: Skyhorse Publishing, 2016.

Hitchens, Christopher. *Thomas Jefferson, Author of America.* HarperCollins, 2005.

Holowchak, M. Andrew. *Framing A Legend: Exposing the Distorted History of Thomas Jefferson and Sally Hemmings.* Amherst, New York: Prometheus Books, 2013.

Johnson, Paul. *A History of the American People.* New York: HarperPerennial, 1998.

Ledeen, Michael A. *Tocqueville on American Character.* New York: St. Martin's Press, 2000.

Lewis, Jo H., and Gordon Palmer. *What Every Christian Should Know.* Wheaton, Illinois: Christianity Today / Victor Books, 1989.

Lutzer, Erwin. *When A Nation Forgets God: 7 Lessons We Must Learn From Nazi Germany*. Chicago, Illinois: Moody Press, 2016.

Machen, J. Gresham, and John W. Robbins. *Education, Christianity, and the State*. Unicoi, Tennessee: Trinity Foundation, 2004.

Marshall, Peter. *The Light and the Glory*. Old Tappan, New Jersey: Fleming H. Revell Publishers, 1977.

Marshall, Peter, and David Manuel. *From Sea to Shining Sea* (sequel to *The Light and the Glory*). Old Tappan, New Jersey: Fleming H. Revell Publishers, 1986.

Muncy, Mitchell S., ed. *The End of Democracy? A Crisis of Legitimacy*. Dallas, Texas: Spence Publishing, 1999.

Noll, Mark A. *A History of Christianity in the United States and Canada*. Grand Rapids, Michigan: Wm. B. Eerdman's Publishing Company, 1992.

Rawlings, J. Steven. *Legal Strategies to Defend Biblical Truth*. Dubuque, Iowa: Kendall Hunt Publishing, 2017.

Sandoz, Ellis, ed. *Political Sermons of the American Founding Era*. Indianapolis, Indiana: Liberty Press, 1991.

Schneider, Richard H. *Freedom's Holy Light*. Carmel, New York: Guideposts Publishing, 1985.

Schweikart, Larry. *48 Liberal Lies About American History (That You Probably Learned In School)*. New York: Sentinel/Penguin, 2008.

Shapiro, Ben. *Brainwashed: How Universities Indoctrinate America's Youth*. Nashville, Tennessee: Thomas Nelson, 2010.

Starnes, Todd. *Culture Jihad—How to Stop the Left from Killing a Nation*. New York: Post Hill Press, 2019.

Stark, Rodney. *America's Blessings: How Religion Benefits Everyone Including Atheists*. West Conshohocken, Pennsylvania: Templeton Press, 2012.

Sweeney, Douglas A. *The American Evangelical Story*. Grand Rapids, Michigan: Baker Academic, 2005.

Sykes, Charles J. *Fail U.: The False Promise of Higher Education*. New York: St. Martin's Press, 2016.

Turner, John G. *They Knew They Were Pilgrims: Plymouth Colony and the Contest For American Liberty*. New Haven, Connecticut: Yale University Press, 2020.

Wallis, Charles L. *Our American Heritage*. New York: Harper and Row Publishers, 1970.

ABOUT THE AUTHOR

For more than a decade Alex McFarland has been heard daily via the American Family Radio Network's nationally syndicated broadcast *Exploring the Word*. An expert on apologetics and trends within worldview and culture, Alex is a frequent contributor to many colleges, news media outlets, and religious organizations.

As an evangelist, author, and advocate for biblical truth, Alex McFarland speaks worldwide. He has preached in more than 2,000 churches throughout North America and internationally. He also speaks at Christian events, conferences, debates, and other venues to teach biblical truths and preach the gospel.

Alex is a frequent spokesperson on FOX News, and has been interviewed by other media outlets including the *New York Times, Wall Street Journal, The Alan Colmes Show,* "The Strategy Room," Billy Graham's Decision radio broadcast, Family Talk with James Dobson, *Truth & Liberty With Andrew Wommack,* Focus On The Family, NPR's *All Things Considered, Washington Post,* Chuck Colson's *BreakPoint,* BBC, CBN *700 Club,* CBS, NBC, CSPAN, SRN, Billy Graham's *Decision* magazine, *Christianity Today,* and the Associated Press (AP) wire service.

Alex is the only evangelist to have preached in all 50 states in only 50 days. His "Tour Of Truth" crusade swept across America with 64 evangelistic services from which came many decisions to receive Jesus and by which many Christians were equipped and encouraged.

Alex's greatest passion is growing the Body of Christ and instructing believers on how to stand strong for the Christian faith. In the early 1990s, Alex pioneered the *Truth For A New Generation Apologetics* conferences designed to equip teens and adults to know what they believe and why.

The *Truth For A New Generation* conferences feature well-known and respected speakers such as Josh McDowell, Sean McDowell, Lee Strobel, Alveda King, James Dobson, Eric Metaxas, William Federer, Todd Starnes, Frank Turek, Joni Eareckson Tada, Will Graham, Lauren Green, Abraham Hamilton III, Tony Perkins, Ken Ham, David Barton, and many, many others.

Prior to their passing, *Truth For A New Generation* events were honored to feature apologists Ravi Zacharias, Norman Geisler, and Chuck Colson. Such copious vacancies on the evangelical horizon remind us of the importance of continually investing to see God raise up new and committed faith leaders. May God grant that one of those rising Christians leaders will be...*you.*

Fast. Easy.
Convenient.

For the latest Harrison House product information and author news, look no further than your computer. All the details on our powerful, life-changing products are just a click away. New releases, email subscriptions, testimonies, monthly specials—find them all in one place. Visit harrisonhouse.com today!

harrisonhouse.com

OUR VISION

Proclaiming the truth and the power
of the Gospel of Jesus Christ with excellence.
Challenging Christians to live victoriously,
grow spiritually, know God intimately.

CONNECT WITH US ON

Facebook @ HarrisonHousePublishers
and Instagram @ HarrisonHousePublishing
so you can stay up to date with news
about our books and our authors.

Visit us at www.harrisonhouse.com
for a complete product listing as well as
monthly specials for wholesale distribution.